EVERY DAY A
VICTORY

PRACTICAL WEAPONS TO FIGHT, STAND, AND LIVE FREE

WILLIAM WOOD

Chosen
a division of Baker Publishing Group
Minneapolis, Minnesota

© 2023 by William Wood

Published by Chosen Books
Minneapolis, Minnesota
www.chosenbooks.com

Chosen Books is a division of
Baker Publishing Group, Grand Rapids, Michigan

Printed in the United States of America

ISBN 978-0-8007-6292-6 (trade paper)
ISBN 978-1-4934-3939-3 (ebook)
ISBN 978-0-8007-6315-2 (casebound)

Library of Congress Cataloging-in-Publication Control Number: 2022041010

Cover design by Rob Williams, InsideOut Creative Arts, Inc.

Baker Publishing Group publications use paper produced from sustainable forestry practices and post-consumer waste whenever possible.

23 24 25 26 27 28 29   7 6 5 4 3 2 1

"One of the modern voids of Christian writings is on the subject of spiritual warfare. Scripturally, we are admonished to not be unaware of the devil's schemes, yet we often seem to be caught off guard. Sometimes in the modern church world we act as if we are on a cruise line, not on the battle line. William Wood has taken out two birds with one stone—he has exposed the intentions of the enemy and put bullets in our gun against darkness. *Every Day a Victory* is a manual to disciple you to walk in triumph as a lifestyle, while giving you inspiration to be who God created you to be."

Sean Smith, author, *I Am Your Sign* and *Prophetic Evangelism*; www.seanandchristasmith.com

"*Every Day a Victory* is such a liberating and powerful read. William's miraculous testimony of freedom and victory will inspire and bless you! The rich revelations that he shares on how to practically walk out real freedom from fear and shame every day impart hope to readers while empowering them to live in greater and greater levels of freedom, peace, and joy. William lives this message so authentically, and his ministry is filled with powerful demonstrations of what life in the Holy Spirit can really look like. I believe this book will act as a faith injection for readers and will leave them inspired to walk in true freedom and hope."

Katherine Ruonala, senior leader, Glory City Church; founder and facilitator, Australian Prophetic Council; speaker and author

"It is my privilege to recommend to you *Every Day a Victory*. I can recommend this powerful work because I have known the author for many years, first as one of my students at Global School of Supernatural Ministry, then as a powerful minister of the gospel as an associate of Global Awakening. The message of this book is authentic and transparent, because the author has lived it and continues to do so. Your life will be impacted by God as you read this!"

Dr. Mike Hutchings, director of education, Global Awakening; president, God Heals PTSD Foundation

I dedicate this book to my beautiful wife, Chantal Rose Wood. Chantal, you have been my greatest support and encourager in writing this book. You have made so many sacrifices so that I could write. Thank you so much for always being there for me through your love, prayers, and sometimes that needed nudge to keep writing.

I love you!

CONTENTS

FOREWORD

William Wood is a man who values God's Word, the Bible. He devours it, feeds on it, finds hope and direction in it. He also values hearing the *rhema* (spoken word) of God. He understands how both create faith, and he practices his faith in the day-to-day living of life. A life he lives in victory. The first time I heard William speak, it was truly a jaw-dropping moment. As a student at Global Awakening School of Supernatural Ministry, he sat in the back and never pushed himself or a personal agenda. He believed God had sent him to the school and that God was going to give him favor. This quiet student turned into a powerful, dynamic preacher-teacher in seconds. Almost like Clark Kent stepping into the phone booth and Superman stepping out. William had the crowd standing two or three times in ovations for the content and power of his message. None of the other speakers had such an impact on the crowd, including myself.

William's personal story of being brought from death's door and the sovereignty of God in his salvation and healing is mind-blowing. How God taught him principles of living in victory and how William had to adjust to God's leading and teachings indicates he is a willing, humble learner. He is one of the most passionate people I know who preaches the gospel. I have encouraged him to write and am excited to be able to write this foreword for him.

I believe anyone who listens to or reads William's writing will gain insight regarding how to live more victoriously, gain discernment for the enemy's strategies, and gain insight into the ways of God. William is a man of integrity and faith. I highly recommend him and his ministry.

Dr. Randy Clark, author, *Power to Heal*, *Authority to Heal*, *The Healing Breakthrough*, and *Eyewitness to Miracles*; president, Global Awakening Theological Seminary, Family of Faith Christian University

ACKNOWLEDGMENTS

I would like to thank everyone with the Chosen team who has helped me with this book project. You all have been a blessing to work with throughout this entire process.

I would like to thank my spiritual father, Randy Clark, for encouraging me to write a book about the lessons the Lord has taught me. Without his guidance, I might have never started.

I also want to thank everyone throughout my walk with Christ who has helped shape me into the person I am today. There are too many names to list, but you know who you are.

INTRODUCTION

One of the most common questions I am asked while traveling is how I walk in victory. There is a vast difference between getting free and staying free. Getting free is a deliverance from what has kept you bound, while staying free requires a change of beliefs, attitudes, habits, and lifestyle. Many people are open to getting free, but not as many people are open to the responsibility required to stay free.

Over my many years in ministry, only the individuals that have met the challenge of personal responsibility have walked in victory as a lifestyle. This is not to say that those people no longer have struggles. We all live in a broken world filled with drama, trauma, and evil. The difference is that those people no longer allow those struggles to have them. In other words, what happens to us does not have the authority to determine what happens in us unless we give those external things in life that authority. We are the ones who determine our internal environment. We are the ones who need to take responsibility for the person we are on the inside.

My questions to you are these: Are you ready to be a victor? Are you ready to take back your authority? Are you ready to become the person God has designed you to be? If you have answered yes to these questions, then join me in this book to discover that destiny.

PART 1

EXPOSING THE TACTICS AND SCHEMES OF SATAN

1

DISTORTING THE IMAGE OF GOD

When I was a young boy, my favorite cartoon was the *Teenage Mutant Ninja Turtles*. I had a Ninja Turtle costume that I wore every day after school. My mom once sat me down, trying to convince me that the Ninja Turtles were not real. Not only that, she was trying to convince me that I was not a Ninja Turtle.

Of course, I refused to tolerate that. I was fully convinced that I was a Ninja Turtle and the world depended on me to rid it of evil. One day, the school principal called my mom with a problem they were having with me. He informed her that I would dress up like a Ninja Turtle during recess to fight with other kids. When questioned about this, I responded that I was fighting crime in school. The only issue was that I was actually the one creating the crime so that I could be the hero. That's not exactly the way I should have been a protector.

So in essence, the problem child in school was me. My heart was in the right place, but my solutions were creating problems instead of answers. Thinking back on this, as a child, I viewed myself as a solution to the problems of the world. I did not expect anyone else but me to be that. In the same way, we can look at how God created man in the beginning to be a protector within the world.

Picture a world where heaven and earth were designed to overlap and interconnect. This is exactly the original intent of God as found in Genesis 1 and 2. When you study the creation account, you discover so many underlying truths. Together, we will examine two of these truths that I believe are essential to understanding the theme and purpose of creation. In Genesis 1:27–28, we see that God made man in His image to be stewards of His creation. For years, I looked at verse 27 as simply meaning that we resemble God. And while this is true, I don't think that is the only point this verse is communicating.

Consider this statement if you will: We are made in the image of God to be an exact representation of Him in this world. Ephesians 5:1 tells us that we are to be imitators of God. If we are made in His image and are called to be imitators of Him, then it follows that we are designed to reveal God. We are to be an exact expression of His nature to the world and in the world.

I was an associate pastor at a church in Troy, Alabama, when this truth first hit home. One day in church, a gentleman came up to me and began making a lot of off-the-wall statements about what he saw some people doing at church. Then he proceeded to tell me that he was falling away from God because of the actions of these Christians. Without thinking, I replied, "Why are you relating what these Christians are doing to God?" It was a valid question because we are ultimately following

Christ, not man. However, as imitators of God, our actions should reveal God. When we give our lives to Christ, we give up our right to merely represent ourselves. In the same way that we see a reflection of ourselves when we look in a mirror, when we look at Jesus, we should see a clear reflection of who we are to be in the world.

In Genesis 1:28, God blessed man and gave him the responsibility of being stewards of the world He created. I think this reveals two specific things about God's original intent for humankind and for the world. First, we see from this verse that it has been God's intention since creation to work on earth through humankind. That is not to say that He cannot or does not work outside of this. Rather, humankind is just His primary avenue. Jesus confirmed and demonstrated this for us in John 6:38: "For I have come down from heaven, not to do My own will, but the will of Him who sent Me." In this statement, Jesus is showing us that accomplishing the will of God does not come by achievement but through surrender.

The second part of verse 28 reveals a second specific point regarding God's original intent for humankind and the world—God created man to be stewards of this world. God does not create anything without purpose. He has created us with a purpose, and part of that purpose is to bless His creation as we steward it. The condition of the world is our responsibility to manage. Yet many people fail to understand this, so much so that this lack of understanding becomes a stumbling block rather than a revelation of our purpose.

> Accomplishing the will of God does not come by achievement but through surrender.

19

Put another way, when Christ came announcing that the kingdom was at hand, He was inaugurating the plan of redemption for humanity as well as creation. Mathew 28:18–20 echoes Genesis 1:27–28 in that we have been commissioned by Christ to go into *all* the world as His representatives to bring redemption. Once we begin to view "Christ in us" as the answer to the world's problems, then we can begin to bring divine solutions to the world.

What if the majority of darkness in the world is not necessarily a sign of the times but a sign that the people of God do not understand their responsibility as stewards? Back in my hometown, one particular neighborhood was very run down with trash everywhere. I would often go by this neighborhood and find myself extremely annoyed that the people didn't care enough about it to keep it clean.

> What if the majority of darkness in the world is not necessarily a sign of the times but a sign that the people of God do not understand their responsibility as stewards?

One day, as I was complaining about the people, the Lord spoke to me very clearly. "William, set an example for the community to follow." The more I thought about it, the more I realized that God wanted to train me to think about situations differently. He wanted me to see myself as part of the solution. If we don't view ourselves as part of the solution, we can become part of the problem.

Once this realization hit me, I immediately started viewing the people of that neighborhood differently—not as they were but as they were created to be. I started a weekly trash cleanup in the community, as well as visiting each individual home to see if anyone needed prayer. I did this for one year before I started seeing changes in the community itself. After two years, I had led over two hundred people to the Lord. And the people within the community started to clean up their own yards, streets, parks, and homes. While this is obviously a very small victory in the grand scheme of things when compared to the conditions of our present world, this mindset is exactly what we need if we are going to effect change in society.

So what does all this have to do with living in victory? When God originally created humankind, He gave to man His (God's) very own nature, which means that man did not originally have a sinful nature nor was humankind prone to sin. So how did we go from vessels of God's nature to our present sinful nature? How did Satan get Adam and Eve to sin?

Genesis 3 contains the answer for us and also reveals the blueprint that Satan continues to use today. Remember, Satan is not a creator, only a perverter. He cannot create; he can only manipulate what has already been created by God. Before we turn to Genesis 3, let me paint the backdrop one more time. Man was completely without sin at creation, completely free from evil. In the garden, everything Adam and Eve knew came directly from God. Against this backdrop, the deceiver came in to corrupt and pervert God's perfect creation. This is why we need to be born again.

> Now the serpent was more cunning than any animal of the field which the LORD God had made. And he said to the woman, "Has God really said, 'You shall not eat from any tree of the garden'?" The woman said to the serpent, "From the fruit of the trees of the garden we may eat; but from the fruit of the tree

which is in the middle of the garden, God has said, 'You shall not eat from it or touch it, or you will die.'" The serpent said to the woman, "You certainly will not die! For God knows that on the day you eat from it your eyes will be opened, and you will become like God, knowing good and evil." When the woman saw that the tree was good for food, and that it was a delight to the eyes, and that the tree was desirable to make one wise, she took some of its fruit and ate; and she also gave some to her husband with her, and he ate. Then the eyes of both of them were opened, and they knew that they were naked; and they sewed fig leaves together and made themselves waist coverings.

Now they heard the sound of the LORD God walking in the garden in the cool of the day, and the man and his wife hid themselves from the presence of the LORD God among the trees of the garden. Then the LORD God called to the man, and said to him, "Where are you?" He said, "I heard the sound of You in the garden, and I was afraid because I was naked; so I hid myself." And He said, "Who told you that you were naked? Have you eaten from the tree of which I commanded you not to eat?" The man said, "The woman whom You gave to be with me, she gave me some of the fruit of the tree, and I ate." Then the LORD God said to the woman, "What is this that you have done?" And the woman said, "The serpent deceived me, and I ate."

Genesis 3:1–13

For many years, all I could see as I read through this passage was that Adam and Eve rebelled against God. While that is true, it didn't dawn on me that the blueprint for Satan's schemes was right in front of my eyes, a blueprint he still uses today. He now has many different versions of this scheme, but it is still the same scheme. I used to think his schemes were so advanced that I might never figure them out, but that is not the case. His schemes are not complicated. Before we move forward, take a moment, reread these verses, and look for the tactics of Satan.

Did you notice that Satan only comes against us in two ways? Everything that Satan does falls into two categories—*deception* and *temptation*. It took me several years to figure out how exactly these two categories do so much damage, but this knowledge gave me a starting point. This is exactly what I want to share with you now—a starting point to walking in freedom in your own life. Knowledge is one thing. Walking out the truths that we are going to unpack in the remainder of this book is another. It will require daily partnership with God. Remember, God intends to work through His people, not just for His people. So with that being said, let's first define *deception* and *temptation* and then break them down within the text itself.

Deception

Scripture reveals that deception dwells where ignorance lives. In other words, the lifeline to deception is ignorance, and it is a powerful lifeline. The Word tells us that ignorance is an absence of understanding or knowledge. "My people are destroyed for lack of knowledge. Since you have rejected knowledge, I also will reject you from being My priest. Since you have forgotten the Law of your God, I also will forget your children" (Hosea 4:6).

In context, this text is a rebuke to Israel for rejecting the law that revealed the will of God and the standard of living by being ignorant of it. This verse reveals that ignorance is the first step to destruction. Today, Satan's aim is to take advantage of our ignorance to bring destruction in our lives. Any place where there is lack is a knowledge issue.

Many so-called truths are out there, but a lack of understanding of God's truth is what empowers the voice of Satan in our lives. In the Gospel of John, Satan is defined as the father of lies (John 8:44). John also says that we shall know the truth and the truth will set us free (John 8:32). Therefore, our bondage to sin is a byproduct of a lie believed, and the lifeline of Satan's lies is ignorance of *God's* truths. Think about it—Satan is not the greatest enemy of our destiny; our rejection of God's truths inhibits our destiny. In other words, the lies of Satan are not what keep us from fulfilling our destiny; rather, the ignorance of God's truth keeps us bound from walking out His will in our lives. Satan is a defeated foe that only gains power in our lives through human agreement.

> A lack of understanding of God's truth empowers the voice of Satan in our lives. Satan is not the greatest enemy of our destiny; our rejection of God's truths inhibits our destiny.

About fifteen years ago, when I first began to discover the power of the gospel, particularly in regard to healing, I became violently ill one day with vomiting and diarrhea. This went on for several hours, but I was convinced that the Word of God had an answer for me. As I started going through the Scriptures, I came across a powerful passage in Isaiah 53:5 that decreed that by Christ's wounds, we are healed. This truth had never occurred to me until that very moment. Suddenly, I realized that healing is an accomplished truth.

I immediately stood up and started decreeing this over my body. I did this for almost two hours until finally the sickness lifted. It felt as if a person lifted off me. In other words, the sickness was a demon itself.

This is not to say that every sickness is the physical presence of a demon. However, I came away from this experience with a valuable truth learned that Satan leverages our ignorance of God's truth by implanting his lies. That is why it is so vitally important that we not be ignorant of the truths of God.

For example, in John 13:2, Satan put it into the heart of Judas to betray Jesus. If Judas would have been fully convinced of who Christ was, Satan could not have found an access point in him. The access point Satan looks for is the mind. The mind functions as a gateway into our life, and truth functions as the gatekeeper. Later, in John 13:27, you see that Satan fully entered Judas with his spirit. Satan will first implant a lie for the purpose of creating a place for a spirit to occupy later. This is how strongholds are formed in us. Consider this passage of Scripture:

> For though we walk in the flesh, we do not wage battle accord-ing to the flesh, for the weapons of our warfare are not of the flesh, but divinely powerful for the destruction of fortresses. We are destroying arguments and all arrogance raised against the knowledge of God, and we are taking every thought captive to the obedience of Christ.
>
> 2 Corinthians 10:3–5

Notice this text uses the term "stronghold," which represents a "structure" or "fortress." This text reveals that these structures are formed in us through the gateway of the mind. So Satan sends a thought for the purpose of creating within us a structure to house his presence. Once his presence fills that structure, now the belief system is demonically empowered.

Another consideration is that sometimes the body of Christ has trouble discerning whether physical manifestations are good or evil. Often as believers, we become afraid of manifestations instead of seeing what God is doing in the midst of a divine setup.

> Satan sends a thought for the purpose of creating within us a structure to house his presence. Once his presence fills that structure, now the belief system is demonically empowered.

A few years ago, my wife and I were ministering at a conference. During one of the sessions, a young lady began to physically manifest with shaking and weeping. This manifestation was demonic, although the people surrounding her thought it was a manifestation of the Holy Spirit.

Oftentimes, the Holy Spirit will touch people with a similar physical manifestation. Keep in mind if there is an authentic physical manifestation, then there will be a counterfeit physical manifestation. Satan tries to mimic the Holy Spirit, not the other way around. So with that said, when people begin to manifest the demonic, the light might be exposing the darkness in order to bring healing and freedom to that person.

My wife, Chantal, walked over to the young woman and asked, "Are you ready for freedom?"

She responded, "Yes, I don't feel like these manifestations are of the Lord."

Second Corinthians 3:17 says, "Now the Lord is the Spirit, and where the Spirit of the Lord is, there is freedom." In the case of this young woman, truth was exposing the lies believed.

Years prior, she had what she believed was an angelic vision in which what appeared to be an angel instructed her to change her name. The angel happened to be Satan appearing as an angel of light (2 Corinthians 11:14). The moment she changed her name, she gave access to the deception. This is why Scripture instructs us to test every spirit (1 John 4:1–4). Because this young lady was ignorant about testing the spirit, she gave place to Satan's lie. Using this text, Chantal commanded the spirit to reveal itself and come out.

The second category Satan comes against us with is temptation.

Temptation

As a young believer, I had a radical conversion from a life of alcohol and drugs and became a completely different person overnight. Even though I experienced a tremendous amount of freedom at once, I still struggled with this one area in my life for a very long time. I would often find myself battling with lustful thoughts.

One night, as I was lying in bed, suddenly, overwhelming emotions and thoughts of lust hit me. At that moment, I realized that these were not my emotions or thoughts. They were coming from a spirit, not from my own desires. I immediately screamed, "No!" with violent authority. As soon as this statement came out of my mouth, the extreme emotions and desires stopped. What I understood in that moment was that Satan tempts us by projecting his sinful nature upon us. I knew immediately that all those times of battling lust in my mind were actually caused by a spirit projecting its own desires upon me, hoping that I would come into agreement with those desires.

Let's look at it another way. When a spirit of fear comes against you, you experience fear because the spirit itself is afraid. Fear is being projected upon you, not produced by you. The objective of Satan is to project his own desires upon you, hoping you will agree with those perverted desires. So at this point, you may be thinking, *How can I discern my emotions from a demonic spirit?* First, for me, it does not come by focusing on the demonic but by identifying the function of the Holy Spirit.

Satan tempts us by projecting his sinful nature upon us.

> But the fruit of the Spirit is love, joy, peace, patience, kindness, goodness, faithfulness, gentleness, self-control; against such things there is no law. Now those who belong to Christ Jesus crucified the flesh with its passions and desires.
>
> Galatians 5:22–24

Notice that these texts reveal nine fruits of the Holy Spirit. This means when we are governed by the Spirit, these nine fruits become our state of being. The moment I encounter an emotion that contradicts one of these nine fruits, I immediately deny it access into my life. I deny it access by not taking ownership of it. Remember that the demonic in our lives is empowered by human agreement. No agreement, no empowerment. So when you feel depression, anxiety, or whatever else contradicts the Spirit, deny it access by not claiming it as yours. Use your voice, speak to the emotion, and tell it to leave. A lot of people are governed by their emotions instead of by the Word. That is why their lives are up and down—because emotions are not stable leaders.

"Submit yourselves, then, to God. Resist the devil, and he will flee from you" (James 4:7 NIV). Notice this text says to resist the devil. The word *resist* means to "actively stand against." Satan is only interested in people he can influence. When he knocks on the door of your heart and finds no agreement, he will flee. This is and should be the normal posture of Satan in our lives: fleeing from us.

Second, I focus on renewing my mind. The renewal of the mind is the first step to being governed by the Spirit. Consider this passage: "For the mind set on the flesh is death, but the mind set on the Spirit is life and peace" (Romans 8:6).

To be governed by the Spirit is a mindset—or what the mind is set on. So to be Spirit-minded means to be Word-minded. When we focus on renewing our minds according to the Word of God, we are bringing our will under the rule of the Spirit. In John 6:63, Jesus declares that His words are spirit. Second Timothy 3:16 declares that "all Scripture is inspired by God." Based on these passages, we see that the Word of God is spiritual truth. So to be governed by the Word is to be governed by the Spirit.

Now, before I move forward, understand that I am speaking of how the enemy tempts us. We also have our desires that need sanctifying and submitting to God. Scripture talks about how we can be carried away into sin by our own desires.

No one is to say when he is tempted, "I am being tempted by God"; for God cannot be tempted by evil, and He Himself does not tempt anyone. But each one is tempted when he is carried away and enticed by his own lust. Then when lust has conceived, it gives birth to sin; and sin, when it has run its course, brings forth death.

James 1:13–15

This is a very revealing text. First, God is not the one tempting people to sin. He will not condone sin. Anyone who says that God leads them into sin is deceived. Second, people fall into sin by their own lust. The word *lust* here means "strong desire." Strong desire comes by the meditation of the mind. Proverbs 23:7 says that as a man thinks within himself, so he is. The Bible connects our state of being to the meditation of our minds. The strong desire that produces sin in our lives comes by meditating on things that are contrary to God's nature. You will not fall into any sin you don't first meditate on. All sin is premeditated. Third, this text reveals that sin is conceived by strong desire. Sin does not come on us like a seizure; it comes by continually meditating on it in our minds.

So as we prepare to go through the truths found in the Genesis 3 account, keep these concepts of deception and temptation in mind.

At the end of each chapter, I've included a prayer and section entitled "Weapons for the Battle." I encourage you to say each prayer out loud and then use the tools that will help you make every day a victory.

PRAYER

I plead the blood of Christ over my mind and emotions. I command every thought to come into agreement with truth and every emotion to come into agreement with the fruit of the Spirit. In Jesus's name.

WEAPONS FOR THE BATTLE

1. How can you recognize deception? Truth exposes deception. When you get the truth of God's Word in your heart, you are gradually molded into a person of discernment. You don't need to study the counterfeit (lies) to be able to discern it. The best way to recognize deception is to become so familiar with the authentic (truth) that you recognize anything that contradicts it. Read your Bible. Start with a chapter a day. The Gospels are a great place to begin, as they focus on the life of Jesus.

2. How can you recognize temptation? When you focus on being led by the Spirit, you will function with the fruit of the Spirit as your guide.

   a. Recognize that not every thought that comes to mind is from you. If it contradicts the fruit of the Spirit, do not give it place in your mind or heed it.

   b. To combat temptation, speak out loud to the temptation and command it to leave. The weapon of truth flows through the avenue of your voice. Find and declare a Scripture in the opposite spirit of what is attacking you. For example, if you are being tempted to be afraid, say, "Spirit of fear, go in Jesus's name because God has not given me a spirit of fear but of power, love, and a sound mind" (see 2 Timothy 1:7). "The LORD is my light and my salvation. I will not fear!" (see Psalm 27:1).

2

LOOKING AT THE FACTS
AND NOT THE TRUTH

With an understanding of deception and temptation, let's take a verse-by-verse look at Genesis 3:1–13. Remember, deception and temptation are the root of everything Satan does.

> Now the serpent was more cunning than any animal of the field which the LORD God had made. And he said to the woman, "Has God really said, 'You shall not eat from any tree of the garden'?"
>
> Genesis 3:1

We need to gather two specific points from this verse. First, the serpent is referred to as the most "cunning" of all the other beasts. Whether you believe the serpent represents Satan himself or not is not the point here. What is obvious is that the deceptive plan operating through the serpent is Satan. Think of Satan as an illusionist, which best describes his personality and nature. He is the father of lies (see John 8:44).

When I was a kid, I loved watching illusionist shows on TV. I was always blown away by how real everything appeared. One day, after watching one of these shows, I noticed another show in the TV guide entitled *Exposing Illusionist*. Intrigued, I watched that show too. When I saw how the illusions were performed, my amazement dissolved. After that, illusions lost their hold on me. Satan is a master at creating illusions and false realities, seeking to capture our imaginations. What makes an illusion real is our belief in the illusion itself. The lifeline of Satan's illusion is human agreement. The first part of this book is aimed at exposing the master illusionist and his deceptive nature so you don't agree with his lies. He is not in the place of authority in your life unless you agree with him.

> Satan is a master at creating illusions and false realities, seeking to capture our imaginations. What makes an illusion real is our belief in the illusion itself.

Second, Satan asked Adam and Eve a question that undermined the command of God. Satan is always seeking our attention so that he can implant his lies in our minds, causing us to listen to him and not to God. Look at what Scripture says about the voice of Christ. "So faith comes from hearing, and hearing by the word of Christ" (Romans 10:17). The voice of Christ contains the seed of faith. Every time we give our attention to the voice of God, faith is produced in us. So if this is true about the voice of God, what does this reveal about the voice of Satan? The voice of Satan contains the seed of unbelief. The serpent spoke to Eve because he was seeking her attention. Once she paid attention to his voice, the seed of unbelief was planted.

Facts versus Truth

You may be asking yourself at this point, *How does the enemy do this in my life without detection?* The most common way that I have found in my own life is that Satan is a master at getting us to look at facts and not truth. Facts and truth are not necessarily the same thing. Every truth is a fact, but not every fact is a truth. Jesus is the personification of truth revealed through His Word. Therefore, anything that is not in alignment with the Word of Christ is a fact seeking the validity of truth.

For example, Satan will wait until you are sick and then whisper in your ear, "Did God *really* say that by His wounds you are healed?" The fact is that you are not feeling well. The truth is that you are whole in Jesus's name. Satan will wait until you are in financial difficulty and whisper, "Did God *really* say that He will provide for you, according to His riches in glory?" The fact is that you don't have the money in your hands at this moment to pay a bill, but the truth is that God will provide for all your needs.

> Satan is a master at getting us to look at facts and not truth.

Satan is a master at getting us to look at the facts of life instead of the truth of God. The aim of the tempter is to displace God's voice with his voice. Let's turn to a passage of Scripture to illustrate this point.

Now an angel of the Lord appeared to him, standing to the right of the altar of incense. Zechariah was troubled when he saw the angel, and fear gripped him. But the angel said to him, "Do not be afraid, Zechariah, for your prayer has been heard, and your wife Elizabeth will bear you a son, and you shall name him John. You will have joy and gladness, and many will rejoice over his birth. For he will be great in the sight of the Lord; and he will drink no wine or liquor, and he will be filled with the Holy Spirit while yet in his mother's womb. And he will turn many of the sons of Israel back to the Lord their God. And it is he who will go as a forerunner before Him in the spirit and power of Elijah, to turn the hearts of the fathers back to their children, and the disobedient to the attitude of the righteous, to make ready a people prepared for the Lord."

Zechariah said to the angel, "How will I know this? For I am an old man, and my wife is advanced in her years." The angel answered and said to him, "I am Gabriel, who stands in the presence of God, and I was sent to speak to you and to bring you this good news. And behold, you will be silent and unable to speak until the day when these things take place, because you did not believe my words, which will be fulfilled at their proper time."

Luke 1:11–20

Although often overlooked, this is one of my favorite stories in the Bible. It illustrates the difference between truth and facts. In this story of the parents of John the Baptist, Zechariah is performing his priestly duties, and he has an angelic visitation from Gabriel. Gabriel has come to Zechariah in response to his petition with a prophetic decree directly from God.

Now, let me stop here for just a moment and ask you a question. If you had Gabriel appear to you with a prophetic word from God, would you believe it? What transpires in this story is hilarious in one aspect and a sad reality in another. Gabriel gives this absolutely profound prophetic word about the birth and mission of Zechariah's son. Instead of excitement, the first thing that comes out of the mouth of Zechariah is unbelief.

Every time I read this passage, I think, *How can he doubt this word?* And then it hits me—I do the same thing all the time. God will speak to me, and while it is obvious to everybody else in my life that God is speaking to me, I go around in circles, wondering if what I am hearing is really from God. I keep asking God to give me confirmation even when I know He has clearly spoken. You know what that really is? It is me seeking an opportunity to be disobedient.

Zechariah then follows up his statement of unbelief by reciting the facts of his life to Gabriel. He is allowing the facts to undermine the truth of his destiny. His response shocks Gabriel to the point that he follows up with this statement: "You will be silent and unable to speak until the day when these things take place, because you did not believe my words, which will be fulfilled at their proper time" (v. 20).

This line of communication is absolutely profound to me. This response from Gabriel reveals that if Zechariah had been able to talk, his words would have aborted his promise. So many times in life, we allow the facts to prophesy to our promise instead of allowing the promise of God to prophesy to the facts. We should never allow the facts to become the prophetic voice of our destiny.

> We should never allow the facts to become the prophetic voice of our destiny.

From this passage, I have learned that if I can't say anything in faith, it is better for me to remain silent. In such a situation, my silence will have more authority than my voice. This is why Satan wants us to be factual instead of truthful. Satan wants us to be ignorant of the truth of God so that our ignorance gives place to his voice. Now remember, this is just one aspect of how Satan comes against us. Remember, Satan is seeking our attention so that he can implant the seed of unbelief. This is where the downfall of man began and where downfall will begin in your life when your attention is captured by Satan.

How Deception and Temptation Function

Let's go back to Genesis 3 to see how Satan's deception and temptation progresses in function.

> The woman said to the serpent, "From the fruit of the trees of the garden we may eat; but from the fruit of the tree which is in the middle of the garden, God has said, 'You shall not eat from it or touch it, or you will die.'"
>
> Genesis 3:2–3

Here, we start to see how the lies of the enemy progress. First, Eve makes the very costly mistake of beginning a conversation with Satan about what God said. We should never allow Satan to bait us into a conversation about anything, let alone the things of God. (His aim in doing that is to redefine what we know to be truth.) When we converse with Satan, our attention gives place to his presence in our life. Satan is only interested in people he can influence, and the first sign he looks for is our attention. So don't even give him a glance.

When I first became a Christian, I was extremely focused on Satan for the first two years of my salvation because I wanted to see his works destroyed in my city. I didn't realize at the time that I was more concerned with Satan and what he was doing than with Christ and what He was doing. This was a vital mistake on my end because I went through hell during this two-year period.

Why? The attention I was giving Satan was giving purpose to his existence in my life. While studying the life of Jesus in the Gospels, it finally dawned on me that nowhere in Scripture do we read about Jesus going from village to village looking for what the devil was doing. Jesus was always and only looking for what the Father was doing. Now, when the devil got in the way, Jesus dealt with him, but Jesus predominantly destroyed the works of the devil by establishing the kingdom of God. He was always preoccupied with the Father, not the devil. Clearly, we need to be aware of the enemy while not being consumed by him.

James 4:7 (NASB95) says, "Submit therefore to God. Resist the devil and he will flee from you." So how do we resist the devil? We resist the devil by submitting to God. When we submit to God, we are yielding to a superior

> We need to be aware of the enemy while not being consumed by him.

force. Your submission to God communicates to Satan that you are not going to enter into his process of deception.

Once he sees that he does not have your attention, the Bible says he will flee from you. The flip side of this is if you give him attention, just like a master illusionist, Satan will then distract you with whatever trick he has up his sleeve. In Eve's case, Satan displaced the truth of God with a lie. This brings me to my second point. Eve added to what God decreed, giving Satan the signal that his lies were implanted in her. Eve didn't realize the reason she added to the command of God was because Satan's implanted lie was twisting God's command within her thinking.

Here is what God actually decreed about the tree. "But from the tree of the knowledge of good and evil you shall not eat, for in the day that you eat from it you will surely die" (Genesis 2:17 NASB95). Notice that God didn't mention anything about touching the tree. Eve chose to add this to her own account.

> Whenever we add or take away from what God has said, it is a sign that a lie has crept in and is twisting our understanding of God's truth.

Here, Satan could see that the seed of unbelief had been planted. Whenever we add or take away from what God has said, it is a sign that a lie has crept in and is twisting our understanding of God's truth. In Genesis 3:4–5 (NASB95), we see the extreme danger of giving attention to Satan. "The serpent said to the woman, 'You surely will not die! For God knows that in the day you eat from it your eyes will be opened, and you will be like God, knowing good and evil.'" Keep in mind that Satan's lies come in seed form and need to be planted in our minds to produce the fruit of deception.

The Progression of Deception

Let's look at three points about these verses. First, Satan downplayed the consequences of sinning against God by insinuating to Eve that God was withholding something good from her.

This is a major point for us to be aware of in the progression of deception. Satan is a master at redefining the consequence of sin by attacking the nature of God. He does this by getting us to disobey God in seemingly insignificant acts. Those acts desensitize us to God. I know this to be true from my own experience.

At one point, I lived in a communal house with about thirty other people. At the time, I was attending a ministry school along with the others in the house. Overall, living there was a wonderful experience except that we all shared the pantry space in the kitchen. This meant that everyone had limited space to store goods. At the time, I worked a job and came home late at night when all the grocery stores nearby were closed. Now, I love to eat a peanut butter and honey sandwich before I go to sleep.

One night, I came in to make my sandwich and realized that I was out of honey. I noticed that my neighbor had a jar of honey in his pantry space right beside mine. I started thinking that it wouldn't hurt if I just took a little honey for my sandwich because it was only just a little bit. I ended up standing there for about ten minutes, wrestling with whether to take something that didn't belong to me.

That's when God spoke very clearly to my heart. "William," He said. "What appears insignificant in the natural carries great significance in the spiritual." When I heard this, I realized that if I gave in to this temptation, it would result in greater temptation later. Everything Satan does is progressive. He starts with subtle acts that become strongholds later.

Satan is very subtle in getting us to disobey God. Ephesians 4:27 tells us, "Do not give the devil an opportunity." We need to be aware of the subtle temptations of Satan that contain delayed destruction. While we don't necessarily see the immediate consequence of the sin, the process of death begins the moment we give in to the temptation. To that point, consider Romans 6:23: "For the wages of sin is death, but the gracious gift of God is eternal life in Christ Jesus our Lord." Eve discovered later, after her initial sin, that although she didn't die immediately, the process of death had begun with that one sin against God. Sin is the ultimate anti-creation plan of destruction. When we engage in sin, we become partakers of the process, the end result being death.

> Sin is the ultimate anti-creation plan of destruction. When we engage in sin, we become partakers of the process, the end result being death.

This leads me to my second point in this passage—Satan projects his desire to be God upon Eve. How did I come to this conclusion? Remember, Satan tempts us by projecting his own desires and nature upon us. Isaiah 14 tells us that all Satan wanted was to be like God. Since Satan could not be like God, he took it upon himself to convince Eve that she was not like God either. Then he insinuated that if Eve wanted to be like God, she would have to listen to his (Satan's) advice. This is another anti-creation lie—that you must look to yourself to become like God.

When I first gave my life to the Lord, I was zealous to be like God in every aspect of my life. What I didn't realize was that in order to imitate God, I first needed to look at Jesus. I thought being like God meant that I needed to get extremely introspective and try to find everything in me that needed changing. For almost a year and a half, I always seemed to find something wrong with me.

Then it finally dawned on me that the only person I was focused on was myself. I had become extremely self-centered. You will never be an imitator of God as long as you are the center of attention. Then I had this inspired thought: What if I turned the focus from myself and put it on Jesus? When I began to do that, I discovered that Jesus is a mirror that we look at so that we can see ourselves clearly (see 2 Corinthians 3:18). In other words, when you look in a mirror, you see a reflection of yourself. If you never look in a mirror, then you will never have a good idea of your own reflection. In the same way, when we look at Jesus, we can clearly see our true reflection the way God created us to be.

> When we look at Jesus, we can clearly see our true reflection, the way God created us to be.

In the case of Eve, we know from Genesis 1 that Eve was already like God because He created her in His image. Yet once the lies of Satan were firmly embedded in her thinking, she didn't realize she was disillusioned about her own design. If Satan can cause you to work to become like who you already are, then you will engage in a never-ending battle. You can spend the entirety of your life trying to become like God when you are already made in His image instead of simply looking at Jesus to see yourself.

This leads me to my third point—that Satan convinced Eve that in order to become like God, she needed to partake of another source of knowledge. Everything Eve knew about herself, creation, and all of life was already coming to her directly from God, and Satan knew this. He also knew that the way to redefine her understanding was to connect her to another source of knowledge, the knowledge of good and evil. Many people fall into this trap of Satan's. When you pursue this other source of knowledge, what you know will be defined by Satan. He will convince you that you have discovered a secret knowledge about God when, in reality, you have been pulled into a world of deception and destruction that masks itself as self-enlightenment.

Several years ago, a guy approached me one day with what he considered to be an enlightened thought. He proceeded to tell me that he discovered that when he smoked a joint before reading the Bible, he received so much more revelation. I assured him that was a bad idea and that he was going down a wrong path. Six months later, I bumped into him again and asked how he was doing. It turned out that he was no longer a believer in Christ and had fully given himself to drugs. You probably would have recognized this tactic as coming from Satan. Yet this happens every day to believers who allow themselves to be pulled into other sources in an effort to get to know God. This is because Satan plays on our desire to be like God.

Watch Out for Satan's *If*

Now we come to verse 6, where the deceptive nature of Satan working within Eve is at its climax.

> When the woman saw that the tree was good for food, and that it was a delight to the eyes, and that the tree was desirable to make one wise, she took from its fruit and ate; and she gave also to her husband with her, and he ate.
>
> Genesis 3:6 NASB95

At this point, a new nature was birthed within Eve. Notice that Eve never once looked at this tree as desirable for food until that moment. Deception caused her to desire what was once undesirable. The lie that she believed was creating new desires within her. The desires she was beginning to have were not coming from her; they were coming from the lie implanted by Satan. Satan's aim is to birth his nature in our lives through his lies. When we believe lies, we give them the power of truth. Satan is seeking human agreement with whatever he does. Through human agreement, he finds his strength.

> Satan's aim is to birth his nature in our lives through his lies. When you believe a lie, you give it the power of truth.

Let's look at Scripture to illustrate this point. Matthew 4 gives an account of Satan tempting Jesus in the wilderness. "And the tempter came and said to Him, "If You are the Son of God, command that these stones become bread" (Matthew 4:3). In this verse, Satan attacks the identity of Jesus in order to usurp His (Jesus's) authority. The aim of Satan was to bring Jesus under his influence so that he could use the authority of Jesus's sonship. Notice he says, "*If You are the Son of God.*"

If Jesus had taken the bait, His authority would have been usurped to authorize the purposes of Satan. You and I are sons and daughters made in the image of God, and Satan is seeking our human agreement to authorize his purposes in our lives. Remember, Satan has no power in us until we come into agreement with him.

This is exactly where Eve was in the Genesis 3 account. Her human agreement authorized the lies of Satan in her life. In essence, she had given Satan purpose. Now that her nature was being changed from the nature of God to the nature of Satan, everything was perverted for her. "Then the eyes of both of them were opened, and they knew that they were naked; and they sewed fig leaves together and made themselves waist coverings" (Genesis 3:7). In many ways, the evil we see in the world reveals the level of human agreement with the works of Satan.

We see from the end of verse 6 that Eve gave some of the fruit from the tree to Adam. This was a critical moment in which Adam was positioned to bring correction to Eve. Instead, he became a partaker of sin. Understand that at this moment, Adam was not the one deceived because he was not the one talking to the serpent. He still knew very well the command of God and the fruit he was not to partake of. "And it was not Adam who was deceived, but the woman being deceived, fell into transgression" (1 Timothy 2:14 NASB95).

According to Scripture, Adam was very aware of the consequences of his actions. I highlight this in order for us to understand the severity of Adam's sin. Eve sinned as a byproduct of deception, but Adam sinned as a byproduct of will. Eve was lured into sin while Adam willfully rejected the command of God. At this moment, they both became partakers of the nature of Satan.

Remember, a lie needs a partner. Satan, empowered through Eve, needed Adam's partnership to launch his plan of anti-creation. Satan needed the human agreement of both Adam and Eve to gain authority in this world. Adam and Eve were co-heirs with each other. Today, we are co-heirs with Christ.

This functions like a joint banking system. In a joint banking system, both parties have full access to the funds. However, in order to transfer the funds to someone else, you need the signature or agreement of both parties. All Satan needed to gain access to their possessions, which was the world, was their agreement. At that point, Satan became the god of this world (see 2 Corinthians 4:4). Thankfully for you and me, Jesus has taken back that authority and made us joint heirs with Him. In other words, the kingdom we have can never be fully taken from us because Jesus will not agree with anything that empowers Satan even though we might.

Now their eyes were open to a new world—the world that Satan wanted them to see. We generally do not see the world as it truly is but as it is through our worldview. This is why God instructs us to constantly renew our minds to conform to the mind of Christ. "And do not be conformed to this world, but be transformed by the renewing of your mind, so that you may prove what the will of God is, that which is good and acceptable and perfect" (Romans 12:2).

This is one of the most profound passages in the Bible. First, we are not to be conformed to this world. Why? Because the values and this world have been reshaped through Satan. Second, we are to be transformed by the renewing of our mind. Why? So that we can reshape this world through God's worldview, which is His new creation. As God's covenant people, we are to be the place where heaven and earth meet. Heaven is not of this world, but it is for this world. As God's people, we are to reshape this world back into the place where heaven and earth interlock and overlap.

PRAYER

God, by Your grace, help me have the eyes to see Your truth over the facts of life. Give me ears to hear Your truth over the opinions of man. And help me have the heart to understand Your truth over the wisdom of this world and the confidence to stand on Your truth as my weapon of warfare. In Jesus's name.

WEAPONS FOR THE BATTLE

1. Remember that Satan uses facts to displace truth. Be aware of what the truth is and be convinced of it. A lie needs a partner, and Satan's empowerment is simply our agreement. Do not agree with him. For example, the facts might say that you have a temperature. But the truth is that the same life that raised Christ from the dead is within you, driving out sickness.

2. Do not disregard little temptations or distractions. Everything is big because giving in now will result in giving in to greater temptation later. For example, someone who shoplifts might gradually move to breaking into houses and stealing and might eventually rob a bank.

3. Be aware of what the enemy is doing but do not focus on it. Give your attention to what Jesus is doing and on building His kingdom. If the enemy starts to get too much of your attention, submit yourself to God so you do not enter Satan's process of deception. Satan will flee when you resist him.

3

FEAR, SHAME,
AND VICTIM MENTALITY

About two months after my salvation, I began attending a Vineyard Church in my hometown. This church became my home church for the next several years. I'm so grateful for the leadership, friends, and community that were formed there. One weekend, we had a prophetic conference where people shared on the gifts of the Holy Spirit and using the gift of prophecy. I had never experienced a prophetic word, so I was extremely excited for what I might receive from the Lord that weekend. The conference began, and everyone around me was receiving a prophetic word, but there was no word for me. That is, until the last day of the conference. I was sitting on the floor next to the front row when a lady called me to stand up. Immediately, my heart began pounding in anticipation of what God might say. To my surprise, this was the word that proceeded to come out of the speaker's mouth in front of the entire church: "You, son, are full of lust and deceit, and you need to get in the Word of God."

As these words proceeded from her mouth, my heart sank into my chest, and this deep desperation to be pleasing to God came over me. Even though at that particular time, none of what she said was accurate, Satan used it to lure me into a place of shame.

I spent the next three months trying to clean myself up for God. Instead of blissful communion with the Lord, I was focused on ridding myself of any sort of lustful tendency. Thankfully, the pastor was very relational and helped me through that season in life, as well as bringing correction to the prophetic word itself. I don't share this story to cast shade on the prophetic nor the person that gave the word. We all must learn how to fail forward. That is just the process of maturating in Christ. I share this story to show the deceptive ways Satan lures us into viewing ourselves from his point of view.

Satan wants to redefine our worldview so that we see everything through his corrupt nature. Once Adam and Eve saw the world as Satan wanted them to see it, the progression of deception continued as they looked at themselves with eyes of shame. Let's look at verse 7 again: "Then the eyes of both of them were opened, and they knew that they were naked; and they sewed fig leaves together and made themselves waist coverings" (Genesis 3:7).

> Satan wants to redefine our worldview so that we see everything through his corrupt nature.

Notice that they never even knew they were naked until that moment. This new way of seeing caused them to be ashamed of their own nakedness because that was the way Satan saw them. The deceptive nature of Satan causes us to view ourselves and the world with

50

his perspective. This is why we need to look at Jesus. When we look at Him, we can see ourselves the way He designed us to be.

At the close of verse 7, notice that with Satan's corrupt vision of the world, Adam and Eve suddenly thought they needed to cover themselves by the work of their hands. They forgot that they were actually covered by God, the One who sanctified them. Satan has opened their eyes to a view that said they needed to cover and purify themselves.

Understanding God as Father

At this point in the narrative, Adam and Eve are fully opened to the world of Satan. He has redefined the way they view themselves so that he can redefine the way they view God. We see this in verse 8. Adam and Eve hear God walking in the garden like He does every day. Yet instead of running to God, they hide from Him. "They heard the sound of the Lord God walking in the garden in the cool of the day, and the man and his wife hid themselves from the presence of the Lord God among the trees of the garden" (Genesis 3:8).

A major sign that someone is fully in the world of deception is when they hide from the only one (God) who can bring correction and justice in their lives. Adam and Eve no longer viewed God as someone they could run to for safety. Now they viewed Him as a judge to hide from. While it is true that God is a judge, He is the God of justice. Satan wants you to view God as a judge of punishment. Justice is about setting things right, whereas punishment is about suffering in and of itself. I am not saying that in God's justice, there will not be suffering. What I am saying is that in God's justice, redemption will always be the end goal. God is always about restoring fellowship with us.

In this particular case, Adam and Eve were not viewing God as our justifier but as our punisher. They were seeing God the way Satan wanted them to see Him. Christians hold this common view of God today without realizing that this view is demonic at its core. Too often, the gospel is unintentionally presented to allow Satan to change the emphasis of John 3:16 to say, "God so hated the world He killed His only begotten Son." This is a picture of an angry, hateful God that needed to be appeased instead of the loving Father who was willing to come in the form of man to set the world back to rights. Here is the best parable to consider when thinking about God as a father.

> In God's justice, redemption will always be the end goal. God is always about restoring fellowship with us.

And He said, "A man had two sons. The younger of them said to his father, 'Father, give me the share of the estate that is coming to me.' And so he divided his wealth between them. And not many days later, the younger son gathered everything together and went on a journey to a distant country, and there he squandered his estate in wild living. Now when he had spent everything, a severe famine occurred in that country, and he began doing without. So he went and hired himself out to one of the citizens of that country, and he sent him into his fields to feed pigs. And he longed to have his fill of the carob pods that the pigs were eating, and no one was giving him anything. But when he came to his senses, he said, 'How many of my father's hired laborers have more than enough bread, but I am dying here from hunger! I will set out and go to my father, and will say to him, "Father, I have sinned against heaven, and in your sight; I am no longer worthy to be called your son; treat me as one of your hired laborers.'" So he set out and came to his father. But while he was still a long way off, his father saw him and felt compassion for him, and ran and embraced him and kissed him. And the son said to him, 'Father, I have sinned against heaven and in your sight; I am no longer worthy to be called your son.' But the father said to his slaves, 'Quickly bring out the best robe and put it on him, and put a ring on his finger and sandals on his feet; and bring the fattened calf, slaughter it, and let's eat and celebrate; for this son of mine was dead and has come to life again; he was lost and has been found.' And they began to celebrate.

"Now his older son was in the field, and when he came and approached the house, he heard music and dancing. And he summoned one of the servants and began inquiring what these things could be. And he said to him, 'Your brother has come, and your father has slaughtered the fattened calf because he has received him back safe and sound.' But he became angry and was not willing to go in; and his father came out and began pleading with him. But he answered and said to his father, 'Look! For so many years I have been serving you and I have never neglected a command of yours; and yet you never gave me a young goat, so that I might celebrate with my friends; but when this son of yours came, who has devoured your wealth with prostitutes, you slaughtered the fattened calf for him.' And he said to him, 'Son, you have always been with me, and all that is mine is yours. But we had to celebrate and rejoice, because this brother of yours was dead and has begun to live, and was lost and has been found.'"

Luke 15:11–32

As you read through this parable, you can see the heart of the father, not just for the one son that left home, but also for the other son that stayed with him. The first son comes to his senses after squandering his inheritance and begins his journey back home. The father has been waiting with great anticipation for his son to return. When the father sees him, notice that he doesn't wait for the son to make it to the house before he runs out and embraces him with a kiss. The father in this parable wasn't waiting to judge and condemn but to restore and redeem. God's heart is for restored fellowship with us, which precedes correction and discipline. Notice also that the other brother is offended at the father's response and does not celebrate his brother's return. Once again, the father didn't go to his son in judgment but with the hope of restoring brotherhood. This parable clearly shows us the heart of God as Father.

Fear and Shame

Let's return to the Garden of Eden in Genesis 3. "Then the LORD God called to the man, and said to him, 'Where are you?' He said, 'I heard the sound of You in the garden, and I was afraid because I was naked; so I hid myself" (Genesis 3:9–10). By the time we make it to these verses, Adam and Eve have been completely reshaped by another world, Satan's world. In verse 9, when God calls out to Adam, "Where are you?" He knows where Adam is, but He is giving Adam an opportunity to come to Him. God was not hunting Adam down like a predator. He was seeking Adam like a father looks for his son. Adam's response is very revealing. His explanation for hiding from God shows two aspects of Satan's world—fear and shame.

Fear and shame are two powerful arrows in Satan's quiver. Notice in this verse that shame precedes fear so that by the time fear appears, shame has already accomplished its work. Dealing with fear doesn't remove shame, but dealing with shame always removes fear. When we try to deal with the fruit of an issue instead of the root of an issue, we simply become experts at managing our pain instead of being freed from it. Freedom isn't being able to handle what happened to you. Freedom is being healed from the trauma it caused.

We now live in a day and time where fear and shame are crippling families, cities, states, and nations. It is time we recognize these tactics of Satan and blow the whistle on them so that people can see the world God intends.

> Fear and shame are two powerful arrows in Satan's quiver. Dealing with fear doesn't remove shame, but dealing with shame always removes fear.

I came out of a life of deep sin and addiction. One of the reasons I have not experienced a tremendous amount of fear and shame throughout my Christian development is simply because the first thing I experienced as a believer was the love of God. I believe that we are changed by being in love with God, but we are not transformed until we realize that He is in love with us. Here is what Scripture says in that regard. "There is no fear in love, but perfect love casts out fear, because fear involves punishment, and the one who fears is not perfected in love" (1 John 4:18). Where fear exists, love is absent. These words resound in my heart after experiencing the Father's piercing love in May 2005, while overdosed on drugs.

At that time of experiencing His love, I was a self-professed atheist. I thought Christianity was nothing but made-up stories to play on the hearts of people. My heart was full of hatred and anger because I saw no future in life. I didn't realize that

I felt dead on the inside because I was denying the existence of God. I thought the best way to escape the pain I felt was to fill myself with drugs and alcohol. However, the more drugs I did, the more drugs I needed to maintain relief. That's the trap you fall into, thinking you can escape your pain. You can never get away from you. You can move to new places, but you will always be there. You will be forced to face you at some point. This is the state I was in when I met God.

I had been on a meth binge without sleep for several days. Unaware to me, my kidneys started failing. The amount of drug and alcohol abuse I suffered for years was also taking a toll on my liver. When I overdosed on drugs, I happened to be walking down the side of a road and fell into a car that knocked me completely out. When I woke back up, I was lying in a hospital bed surrounded by medics saying, "We might lose him."

I passed back out, and when I woke up the second time, several days later, I was in a different hospital. A doctor walked over to me and said, "Your kidneys have completely failed, and your liver is getting weaker. We are doing what we can to help you."

All I could think in that moment was that I would die. I thought that was it for me, dead at only the age of twenty. That night, as I was lying in ICU, this thought entered my mind—*If I could make it just one more day.* So that became my focus every day: to simply wake up the next morning. After several days of this, one night, a bright shining light appeared before my bed. As I looked at this light intently, a figure of a person walked toward me through the light. Within a few moments, this person stepped into the hospital room through this ball of light. Immediately, my entire body began vibrating under this power that I could not explain. At the same time, I felt so much love that I was overwhelmed with comfort. I was just lying there in my bed, shaking and looking at this person and not saying anything. This person sat down on the floor and looked over to the other side of the room. So I followed his gaze.

The wall opened up, and a river of water began to flow right in front of where he was sitting. This person started washing his arms in the water when a voice spoke to me. The voice declared that the water I was seeing would cleanse me if I received Jesus the Christ as Lord and Savior. I responded yes. The vision disappeared, and the power that was upon me went inside me. It was so intense that I fell back out.

The next day, I woke with the doctors shaking me and telling me that they ran tests on me all morning. The function of my kidneys and liver was now completely normal. I don't know if the person I met was an angel or Christ himself. All I know is that I haven't been the same since the love and the power I felt that day cleansed me of my shame and fear. God saved me when I was an atheist and drug addict. He didn't condemn or judge me. He set me free from me. Consider Romans 5:8 in a new light. "But God demonstrates His own love toward us, in that while we were still sinners, Christ died for us."

Jesus died for us while we were sinners. That means He died for us when we were in our most unlovable state, and He still chose us. Jesus literally thinks you are to die for.

Victim Mentality

Back in the garden, the deception continued.

> And He said, "Who told you that you were naked? Have you eaten from the tree of which I commanded you not to eat?" The

man said, "The woman whom You gave to be with me, she gave me from the tree, and I ate." Then the LORD God said to the woman, "What is this you have done?" And the woman said, "The serpent deceived me, and I ate."

Genesis 3:11–13 NASB95

These three verses reveal another stage of the progression of deception. Satan's ultimate goal is to bring you to this stage that Adam and Eve find themselves in here. This is the victim stage. As you notice in this passage, Adam blames Eve for the entire situation, thereby shifting all responsibility from himself. When we develop a victim mentality, we proclaim our innocence by demonizing others. The victim mentality is completely self-centered and anchored in the survival of self at any cost.

Victims reason that they will be excluded from blame because they are not the problem. Any little thing will send them into a tailspin, circling back around to the lie that they are not the problem. This mentality creates a never-ending cycle in which Satan can sit back and watch the show. He doesn't need to do anything because the person's identity and life are now controlled by the lies he has implanted. They have become a living manifestation of the lies they believe. This is exactly where Satan wants us—completely helpless, self-centered, and defeated humans under his rule.

> When we develop a victim mentality, we proclaim our innocence by demonizing others.

At the close of this passage in Genesis, God asks the woman, "What is this you have done?" Her answer is a continuation of the blame game. She now blames the serpent. Eve could have exercised her dominion over the serpent, but she did not. Actually, Adam and Eve had two opportunities to exercise their dominion over the serpent, but they didn't because they failed to understand the vocation they had been given by God, which was to be stewards of creation. Their fall brought consequences to the entire human race. Humankind was expelled from the garden, dominion was shifted to Satan, a curse was released over the land, and deception and suffering became normal parts of life. Do you see the pattern Satan uses to bring us into bondage? Deception and temptation are the two main weapons of Satan, even though they take on many different forms. I pray that in the pages of this book, you find the tools necessary to continue to walk in the freedom Christ brought you into.

At this point, we should identify where shame, guilt, and a victim mentality come from. Obviously, Satan is the originator of those things, but what creates the cycle of them within our lives? When you read through these texts of the fall of humankind, you notice that Satan was very persuasive in getting them to partake of the Tree of Knowledge of Good and Evil. When you look at the function of that tree, this is exactly the way our conscience functions today.

In fact, when Adam and Eve partook of this tree, they became self-conscious instead of God-conscious. Before the moment of partaking of the Tree of Knowledge of Good and Evil, everything they knew came directly from God. However, when they partook of this tree, another source of right and wrong, good and evil, began to function within them. So they felt shame when they noticed they were naked. It came from this other source of knowledge, their newly formed conscience.

Ever since this moment, humankind was born with a con-science. In other words, humankind has the Tree of Knowledge of Good and Evil operating within them by their conscience. It is an instinctive knowledge that governs us. This is why some people are bent toward the evil side of this knowledge while others are bent toward the good side of this knowledge. Today, we process every decision we make through the conscience in our life. Once our thoughts go through our instinctive sense of good and evil, we then make a decision. The conscience functions as our moral guide. However, that guide is not always reliable. In fact, it is only reliable to the degree that it is sanctified accord-ing to the truth of God's Word. This is why we must instruct our conscience through the renewing of the mind. With this, let's look at a few passages of Scripture.

"I speak the truth in Christ—I lie not, my conscience also bearing me witness in the Holy Ghost" (Romans 9:1 KJ21). Notice the conscience bears witness to something. This is the part of us that connects to (or resists) what people are saying or doing. Our conscience responds. In this text, the conscience bears witness to the Holy Spirit. In fact, I'd like to propose that the Holy Spirit guides the life through the conscience, however, only to the degree that we submit our will to the Spirit. We have already established that the first step to being governed by the Spirit comes through the renewal of the mind. What we put into our minds will affect the sensitivity of our consciences and the degree to which they are aligned with the Word of God. The conscience is a moral guide, but it is not always reliable. To ensure our conscience is bearing witness to the right spirit, we must instruct our conscience with truth so that we can trust the convictions we feel. Here is another passage that describes the function of the conscience.

> For when Gentiles who do not have the Law instinctively per-
> form the requirements of the Law, these, though not having
> the Law, are a law to themselves, in that they show the work
> of the Law written in their hearts, their conscience testifying
> and their thoughts alternately accusing or else defending them.
>
> Romans 2:14–15 NASB95

This text describes Gentiles (unbelievers) who do not have the law but who instinctively follow it based on their conscience. Our conscience accuses or defends the decisions we make. So the sense of accusation comes from the conscience. God is not bringing accusation against us. If we feel or sense that within ourselves, we must understand that it is either Satan or our conscience. In fact, Scripture decrees this.

> Who is the one who condemns? Christ Jesus is He who died,
> but rather, was raised, who is at the right hand of God, who
> also intercedes for us.
>
> Romans 8:34

This passage is clear that Christ died on our behalf and is interceding for us. First, that means that He took upon Himself the judgment we deserved so that we can take upon ourselves the mercy He deserved. Second, if Christ is interceding on our behalf, how can He then be condemning us? That sense of condemnation comes from our conscience. To reinforce this point, consider this passage: "Dear friends, if our conscience does not condemn us, we have confidence in the presence of God" (1 John 3:21 NET).

Notice that condemnation or confidence before God comes from the conscience. In this text, God is not the one condemning. The condemnation, along with guilt, shame, and fear, are coming from a guilty conscience. When the conscience has been defiled, it condemns us, which can feel as if it is coming from God. This is important to understand so that we know that when we feel these emotions, they are not coming from God. They are only coming from Satan or our own guilty conscience. Here is the truth: "There is therefore now no condemnation for those who are in Christ Jesus" (Romans 8:1 KJ21).

You may be wondering at this point what you can do to rid yourself of a guilty conscience so that you can live confidently before God. First, we must repent and allow the blood of Christ to cleanse us. Second, we must sanctify the conscience with the truth of God's Word. Third, we must yield our wills to the guidance of the Holy Spirit. Fourth, we must form a self-image that is in Christ. A self-image is simply a mental picture we have of ourselves. Most people do not live in victory because they don't see themselves as victorious. When you learn to see yourself the way Christ sees you, you will have confidence before Him. Let this Scripture purge your conscience.

> But when Christ appeared as a high priest of the good things having come, He entered through the greater and more perfect tabernacle, not made by hands, that is, not of this creation; and not through the blood of goats and calves, but through His own blood, He entered the holy place once for all time, having obtained eternal redemption. For if the blood of goats and bulls, and the ashes of a heifer sprinkling those who have been defiled, sanctify for the cleansing of the flesh, how much more will the blood of Christ, who through the eternal Spirit offered Himself without blemish to God, cleanse your conscience from dead works to serve the living God?
>
> Hebrews 9:11–14

In the next chapter, I will share another parable related to the heart that has revolutionized the way I live. I believe it will give you more insight into how to walk in victory.

Prayer

Lord, I acknowledge that You are not the source of fear and shame. I repent for blaming You for my pain. I turn my heart to You now as my healer. God, I posture my heart so that You can cleanse and purge my conscience by Your blood and truth and bear witness to Your Spirit with boldness and confidence. In Jesus's name.

Weapons for the Battle

1. To start the journey to overcoming fear and shame, first identify the source. These come from two places: Satan, the accuser, or your own conscience that has been wounded, defiled, or seared. Fear and shame do not come from God. He is not the source of your pain. He is the one that can set you free. Second, begin the process of unraveling the lies surrounding the fear and shame. This removes the attachments that are empowering Satan in those areas. Remember, truth is your weapon that unravels the lies. Third, find a solid church or person that can walk with you through the process of healing.
2. To overcome the victim mentality, first take personal responsibility for your own life. Remember that you

cannot control what other people do. You can only control what you do. This is important because it takes the focus off external causes. Second, form a new self-image or mental picture of yourself. Picture yourself as a victor in Christ. It helps you to know that in Christ, you can do all things. Third, change the internal dialogue that you have with yourself. That internal dialogue determines our overall emotional health.

4

How Satan Strips You of Faith

Several years ago, as I was doing a study of the Gospels, I came upon Luke 8:4–15, which is known as the parable of the sower. As I began to look at what this parable was communicating, I started to gain a greater understanding of how God's world works. Let's take a moment to examine an overview of this parable. As we break it down, keep in mind that the kingdom of God is not of this world, but it is for this world. This is important so that we can walk out the reality of the kingdom.

We are told in verse 11 that the seed here represents the Word of God. The parable goes on to give a description of four types of ground or soil that I refer to as four conditions of the heart. The soil in this parable is the heart or mind into which the seed, the Word of God, is planted. This is key to understanding the richness of truth in this parable.

EXPOSING THE TACTICS AND SCHEMES OF SATAN

[Jesus said,] "The sower went out to sow his seed; and as he sowed, some fell beside the road, and it was trampled underfoot, and the birds of the sky ate it up. Other seed fell on rocky soil, and when it came up, it withered away because it had no moisture. Other seed fell among the thorns; and the thorns grew up with it and choked it out. And yet other seed fell into the good soil, and grew up, and produced a crop a hundred times as much." As He said these things, He would call out, "The one who has ears to hear, let him hear."

vv. 5–8

These four conditions of the heart—beside the road, on rocky soil, among thorns, into good soil—represent four different groups of people or four specific stages in a believer's journey. Notice that the same seed was cast on all four types of ground, which means all four types of ground contain the same potential for harvest. So the harvest received was not contingent upon the seed sown but on whether the ground was prepared. This means the main focus we should have is the preparation of our soil. None of us start off as good soil; we gradually become good soil.

If the seed is the Word of God (v. 11) and the soil is the mind or heart, then it follows that all our words are seeds that have the potential to reap a harvest in the "soil" of our mind. Therefore, every thought we have is a seed seeking soil. We should distinguish here between the seed as the Word of God and our own thoughts as seeds. Any thought that does not produce the reality of Christ in our lives is merely a human thought. So not every thought we have is the Word of God. We can have ungodly thoughts. A mind renewed by the Spirit of God will yield godly thoughts or godly seeds.

This reveals that every thought contains the potential of being the prophetic voice of our lives. "For as he thinks within himself, so he is. He says to you, 'Eat and drink!' But his heart is not with you" (Proverbs 23:7). This passage is clear that our state of being and the direction our lives are headed are dependent upon the mediation of our minds. So if you logically think this through, you see the progression of thoughts into harvest. In other words, when you sow a thought, you reap an action. When you sow an action, you reap a habit. When you sow a habit, you reap a lifestyle. When you sow a lifestyle, you reap a destiny.[1] In fact, there is a divine connection between what you are thinking today and what you are fulfilling tomorrow. Your thoughts today are literally the prophetic voice of your destiny tomorrow.

When you look at the seed and the soil in this context, you begin to see the importance of the renewing of the mind, particularly according to Romans 12:2: "And do not be conformed to this world, but be transformed by the renewing of your mind, so that you may prove what the will of God is, that which is good and acceptable and perfect." Verse 2 says that the purpose of the renewing of the mind is to prove the will of

> When you sow a thought, you reap an action. When you sow an action, you reap a habit. When you sow a habit, you reap a lifestyle. When you sow a lifestyle, you reap a destiny.

1. Variations of this progression of thought have been credited to numerous individuals, going back centuries. See "Watch Your Thoughts, They Become Words; Watch Your Words, They Become Actions," Quote Investigator, accessed July 8, 2022, https://quoteinvestigator.com/2013/01/10/watch-your-thoughts.

God. You are designed to think like Christ on the earth. In fact, the renewing of the mind means "becoming awakened to the mind of Christ within you." The more your mind is renewed, the more you understand your vocation as a son or daughter.

First Corinthians 2:16 tells us that if we have the mind of Christ within us, then we contain the thoughts of God. "For who has known the mind of the Lord, that He will instruct Him? But we have the mind of Christ." If we contain the thoughts of God, then we can learn to trust our thoughts as the voice of God. Obviously, this will be true only to the degree we renew our minds according to the Word. The written Word will activate in us the words we speak through the mind of Christ.

Many of you will recognize this type of speaking as an inward intuition or an internal dialogue we have, which means the voice of God can be mistaken for your own voice. This is part of the way God had designed you to hear from Him. You are designed to hear from God and process what you are hearing so that you can perceive what He intends to do on earth. Every one of us has internal dialogue going on within us all day long. You are constantly processing everything you see or hear within yourself. Why not commune with the Spirit that abides within the same way?

Processing Thoughts through God's Perspective

Yet there is a major stumbling block when it comes to hearing the voice of God through our thoughts, and that stumbling block is our logic. In fact, logic often hinders our ability to have our minds renewed. Most people process God through their own logic, but God is asking us to process our logic through

His so that we can think from His divine perspective. When we process God through our own logic, we reduce Him to our level of understanding. In essence, we begin to serve a God formed out of our own human reasoning. On the flip side, when we process our logic through God's divine perspective, we discover the mind of Christ within us, thus establishing fellowship with the Spirit of Christ.

Everything God does is logical according to the reality of His world. When the Lord began to teach me about this particular truth, I had prayed a prayer that went something like, "God, I will do anything you ask even if it doesn't make logical sense." Little did I know that God would be reshaping my understanding of logic as a result of this prayer.

The first time it happened, I was doing street evangelism with my friend Woody. We were on our way home. I was in the passenger seat looking out the window when a black bird caught my eye. As I looked at the bird, I heard in my mind, "direction to death." It was a random thought, but I didn't think it was coming from my mind. When I mentioned it to Woody, he suggested we follow the bird to see what would happen. This was because the only way to find out if the word was from God was to act on it. We grow in our confidence in listening to the voice of God by acting on what we believe He is saying.

As we followed the bird, it flew down a long driveway and landed in a tree above a mobile home. Woody and I pulled into the driveway and were greeted by a man on the porch holding a rifle. I was a little concerned, not knowing why he had a gun. Besides, what would we say to this guy? Were we going to tell him that we followed a bird to his house? Woody rolled down the window, and before I knew what was happening, I blurted out, "We are here because someone is dying."

The man immediately fell to his knees, weeping on the porch. Woody and I got out of the car and asked him what was going on. He told us that his five-year-old son was in the hospital, dying. Woody and I started to pray, and as we did, the power of God came over us. We prayed and cried with this man for a long time. Later, I found out that the moment we prayed for his son, the power of God healed him in the hospital. Wow! If we had processed the voice of God through our own logic, we wouldn't have followed the bird to that man's house.

This experience taught me so much about my thoughts and the voice of God. Our thoughts are so important. If the Word of God is seed and our mind is the soil, then we had better pay proper attention to what we plant in our lives. The same way that we hear the voice of God through thoughts is the same way Satan tries to speak to us as well. Remember, Satan's agenda is different from God's agenda. If our renewed mind can prove God's will, then the unrenewed mind will prove Satan's will. There is a constant battle for the mind because it is where we are shaped into the people we become. We must take responsibility for our thoughts. The mind is the gateway into our lives, and we have control over what we grant access to.

> If the Word of God is seed and our mind is the soil, then we had better pay proper attention to what we plant in our lives.

Consider the following verses:

For though we walk in the flesh, we do not wage battle according to the flesh, for the weapons of our warfare are not of the flesh, but divinely powerful for the destruction of fortresses. We are destroying arguments and all arrogance raised against the knowledge of God, and we are taking every thought captive to the obedience of Christ.

2 Corinthians 10:3–5

Notice that this passage begins by telling us that we do not war according to the flesh. Our warfare is against lofty things raised up against the knowledge of God. The battle is played out in our minds. We can win this battle by taking every thought captive to the obedience of Christ. The Scripture doesn't say "some" thoughts; it says "every" thought. Why? Because God knows that demonic structures are formed in our lives through thoughts. Thoughts are the seeds planted in the soil of our minds. The mind includes three aspects—mind, will, and emotions—as the makeup of the heart. Luke 5:22 (NASB95) gives us further insight into the makeup of our hearts. "But Jesus, aware of their reasonings, answered and said to them, 'Why are you reasoning in your hearts?'" The word "heart" here is referring to the mind. Here, Jesus connects their reasoning to the heart.

With this in mind, let's return to the parable of the sower to discover how the kingdom grows in our lives while exposing how the enemy tries to stop it. Luke 8:12 gets into the meat of the parable. "Those beside the road are the ones who have heard; then the devil comes and takes away the word from their heart, so that they will not believe and be saved." The devil comes to snatch the Word from us so that we will not believe and be saved.

If you are thinking, *I'm already saved, so this verse doesn't apply to me, think again.* That depends on your understanding of salvation. If you believe that salvation is saying yes to Jesus and one day spending eternity with Him and nothing more, then, yes, you will overlook this passage. However, if your understanding of salvation is that when you say yes to Jesus, He also comes to dwell within you now, then you understand that your entire life from that point on is the unfolding of your salvation. Salvation deals with everything Jesus provided through His atonement. Think of it this way. Jesus gave us victory over everything He defeated on the cross. In that context, this passage has a great deal to do with us because it gives insight into the mind of Satan. Satan knows that the Word of God contains the seed of faith, and therefore, he wants to strip us of the faith in our lives that appropriates the benefits of our salvation.

> Satan wants you to become a Christian atheist—someone that believes in Christ but lives as if He doesn't exist. If Satan can't strip you of salvation, then he will aim to strip you of the faith that produces the benefits of your salvation.

Romans 10:17 says that faith comes by hearing, and hearing by the Word of Christ. So if faith comes by hearing the Word of Christ, then unbelief comes by hearing the word of Satan. Let me put it in this context: If you have any area of your life where there is a lack of faith, it may be because you are listening to the wrong voice. You must understand that every time the Word of God is sown into your heart, Satan sees it as an opportunity to strip you of that word because it produces faith. Satan wants you to become a Christian atheist—someone that believes in Christ but lives as if He doesn't exist. If Satan can't strip you of salvation, then he will aim to strip you of the faith that produces the benefits of your salvation.

How Satan Strips You of Faith

Let's take a look at verse 19 from the parable of the sower in the book of Matthew for more clarity on how this plays out—how Satan strips us of the word of faith.

> When anyone hears the word of the kingdom and does not understand it, the evil one comes and snatches away what has been sown in his heart. This is the one sown with seed beside the road.
>
> Matthew 13:19

This verse reveals that anyone that hears the Word of God but does not understand it will find that the evil one snatches it away. In other words, whoever doesn't set their heart to understand the Word of God actually rejects it from being planted in their mind. In this context, Satan strips you of the Word simply because you did not set your heart to understand it. To understand the Word means you are seeking to know how it functions in your life. Consider James 2:20–21 (NET): "But would you like evidence, you empty fellow, that faith without works is useless? Was not Abraham our father justified by works when he offered Isaac his son on the altar?"

Abraham's faith was working together with his works, and his faith was perfected by works. These texts verify that without works, our faith is dead or is not brought to completion. What does this mean? The word *perfected* here means "completed." In other words, what we have received from Christ by faith independent of our works finds its completion in our life through our works. Faith looks like something.

Those who don't seek understanding walk in intentional or willful ignorance, which is a major stumbling block to

Christians. Consider what Scripture has to say to us in this regard.

> My people are destroyed for lack of knowledge. Since you have rejected knowledge, I also will reject you from being My priest. Since you have forgotten the Law of your God, I also will forget your children.
>
> Hosea 4:6

It is vital to set your heart to understand the Word sown in your life if you are to be a person of biblical faith. So how do you know that you're setting your heart to understand the Word that has been sown? Ask yourself the following questions:

- Am I willing to allow the Word of God to transform my thinking?
- Am I willing to allow the Word of God to establish my values?
- Am I willing to allow the Word of God to be expressed through my life?

Let's look at a passage that illustrates this point.

> But prove yourselves doers of the word, and not just hearers who deceive themselves. For if anyone is a hearer of the word and not a doer, he is like a man who looks at his natural face in a mirror; for once he has looked at himself and gone away, he has immediately forgotten what kind of person he was. But one who has looked intently at the perfect law, the law of freedom, and has continued in it, not having become a

forgetful hearer but an active doer, this person will be blessed in what he does.

James 1:22–25

To set your heart to understand the Word that has been sown means allowing it to determine how you live. We must be doers of the Word because any truth that isn't lived out becomes a weapon in Satan's hand to delude us. When we are not living out the Word of God as James 1 suggests, we are like someone that looks in a mirror, sees their identity, and immediately forgets it once they walk away. Truth lived out will establish the Word in our hearts and our identities. Otherwise, we will only know our identity while looking in the mirror.

> Truth lived out will establish the Word in our hearts and our identities.

Look at it this way—there is a difference between believing *in* Jesus and believing Jesus. James 1:25 says that when you abide as a doer, not forgetting the Word, you will be blessed in what you do. When you watch a movie, you have to believe in the movie to enjoy the story. However, you don't believe a movie is a real story that needs to be applied to your life. Yet, many Christians approach the Word of God this way. They simply believe in the Word, which allows them to enjoy the story, but they don't believe the Word that allows the story to reshape their life.

Any truth of God's that isn't lived simply becomes a story of entertainment and not a weapon of warfare against the enemy. Let me repeat that: Truth lived is a weapon of warfare against the enemy. To sum it up, we are to set our hearts to understand, which means to hear and apply the Word to our beliefs, thereby allowing God's Word to affect our actions.

When I was a pastor, I started ministering at the nearby county jail every Sunday. I wanted to reach out to those that were bound in the lifestyle God delivered me out of. I would be able to connect with them in a way that other ministers could not because of my background with drug abuse. I visited this jail for about two years, ministering week in and week out. While people were in jail, they could more easily apply the Word to their lives. They would pray, study the Word, and act on what it said. However, as soon as they got out of jail, everything they were doing to strengthen their faith stopped. After six months to a year, they would be right back to a place of defeat and unbelief.

> Truth lived is a weapon of warfare against the enemy.

This frustrated me so much. I could not understand why someone would go back to that type of lifestyle. Then I realized that Satan stripped them of the Word because they were not faithful in keeping it. When the Word is stripped from us, we are left empty with only a memory of its existence. The reality of the Word is gone. That's why people will say I just don't feel the way I used to. It's because they didn't set their hearts to understand the Word and didn't even know it was stripped from them.

After this realization, I thought I would change my tactics and started allowing people to live with me at my home upon their release. This was a horrible mistake because I quickly realized that most people didn't want to take responsibility for their walk with Christ. They merely wanted to serve God through *my* relationship with Christ. The point is that it is up to us to plant the Word in our lives, to seek to understand how it functions and live accordingly. I am greatly concerned that most people never make it past the first type of soil.

PRAYER

Lord Jesus, I humbly ask for a greater grace to study Your Word. I ask for a greater grace to embrace Your Word with all my heart. I ask for a greater grace to be attentive to Your Word when it is taught. Lord Jesus, I commit today that I will remove all distractions from my mind and heart. In Jesus's name.

WEAPONS FOR THE BATTLE

1. Faith comes by hearing the Word of Christ; unbelief comes by hearing the words of Satan. If Satan cannot get you to reject the Word outright, his aim is to displace it with his voice. He does this by drowning out the voice of God with distractions. Many people allow the voice of the world to be the primary voice they hear through what they watch, read, and listen to daily. Document what you watch, read, and listen to for a week. Then make changes to protect your eyes and ears. Strengthen yourself in the Word and with other godly influences instead. Start by reading or listening to the Word for fifteen minutes a day. Listen to praise and worship music for fifteen minutes a day as well. Increase

the amount of time for both of these. Add reading great Christian books as time allows.

2. Satan attacks the Word through circumstances. Many people embrace circumstances as God testing them, not realizing that they are embracing the agenda of Satan in their lives. God will test you but not through anything that causes sickness or afflictions. The Word will be stripped from you in this area if you fail to realize the difference between God's tests and Satan's attacks. Scripture says that the enemy comes to kill, steal, and destroy (see John 10:10). This criterion describes the work of Satan, not God. Look at what is happening right now in your life. Using these criteria, what is of God, and what is of the enemy? List the following areas: family, friends, church and ministry, work, finances, and physical and mental health. Under each area, write what is happening. Embrace what is of God, and resist what is of the enemy. Apply James 4:7.

5

SHALLOW AND UNGROUNDED

Another tactic of Satan is to attack believers that have no firm root. Luke 8:13 tells us, "Those on the rocky soil are the ones who, when they hear, receive the word with joy; and yet these do not have a firm root; they believe for a while, and in a time of temptation they fall away." They only believe when life is going well. I refer to this type of person as a conditional believer, someone who only believes when the conditions of their life allow them to do so. As soon as those conditions change, so does their allegiance. I am not saying this to be judgmental or condemning but to raise awareness of the tactics of Satan. Understanding the tactics of the enemy is important, but it's more important to develop a deep abiding friendship with God.

Partnering with God

Make no mistake, our adversary, Satan, is on the prowl, looking for someone to devour. The apostle Peter says, "Be of sober spirit, be on the alert. Your adversary, the devil, prowls around like a roaring lion, seeking someone to devour" (1 Peter 5:8). This verse doesn't say the devil *is* a lion, only that he is imitating one because part of his nature is that of a master illusionist.

Since he prowls around like a predator, it follows that he is looking for a specific type of prey. The parable of the seed in Matthew 13 tells us Satan's prey is conditional believers. He doesn't need to manifest himself to this type of believer directly. All he needs to do to come against a conditional believer is to work through circumstances and related issues.

What do I mean by that? Well, first let me be clear that no one should take that statement to the extreme and see every nail you run over in the road as from the devil. We need more discernment than that. Scripture is clear that we are to be people that are governed by the Spirit of God, meaning we are to be internally controlled. When we are internally controlled, our responses to situations are based on Christ within us instead of on the devil who is outside us. A conditional believer is externally controlled. To be externally controlled means that we react to life. Circumstances determine our responses instead of the indwelling presence of Christ.

A family member once loved to make fun of me. This person would look for things in my life to point a finger at and make comments about those. To be honest, it took me a long time to recognize these encounters as tactics of Satan. When I knew I would see that person that day, I immediately started thinking of all the things they were going to say and do. Just thinking about it put me in a bad mood. In other words, I was allowing that person to determine my internal environment. When we are externally controlled, we are giving circumstances the authority of God in our lives. That means what happens to us determines what happens in us.

I soon realized what was happening and that this person was not the issue but Satan through him was. At that moment, I could separate the person from the real enemy. I made a decision that day that I would no longer allow circumstances to determine my life experience. The truth is, we are the ones that control our internal environment. In fact, our internal world is exactly the way we allow it to be. Once I made this decision in my heart, this person's influence immediately lost its power.

> When we are externally controlled, we are giving circumstances the authority of God in our lives.

The next time I saw the person, they started with the comments. But this time, I had no aggression toward them but simply love and compassion. Within a few minutes, the entire situation dissipated, and that person changed toward me from that day forward. The way we respond to a situation reveals who is in control.

Let's return to the parable of the seed from Matthew to understand more of what I mean.

> The one sown with seed on the rocky places, this is the one who hears the word and immediately receives it with joy; yet he has no firm root in himself, but is only temporary, and when affliction or persecution occurs because of the word, immediately he falls away.
>
> Matthew 13:20–21

Notice that it says that the person is "only temporary." They are not firmly rooted in the Word of God and therefore fall away. I think this is a fascinating description as well as a great insight into the purpose of the Word sown.

First, let's explore the statement that this person is only temporary with the Word. This is what was happening to me with my relative: I was not internally controlled by what God was saying. To be internally controlled only comes through continual use of God's Word. This description brings home the point of the necessity of remaining consistent with daily Bible study.

Many Christians tend to view God as someone we worship once a week at church to pay our respects. While we should not neglect assembling together to worship God, our relationship with Him needs to be a daily, ongoing intentional experience. Think about this in terms of relationships you have with people in your life.

The only way you intimately get to know someone is through consistent communication. Communication is key in relationships. One of the top issues that causes conflict in a relationship is poor or a lack of communication. This makes me think about my relationship with my wife. If I only talked to her occasionally, we definitely would not have a very intimate relationship.

Only in deep relationship can you discover someone's heart and motives. Poor communication results in false beliefs about the other person. How many times have you misread someone's actions by projecting your own interpretation onto them, only to find out later that what you perceived was incorrect? I have fallen into that trap many times. When you don't have daily intentional fellowship with God, you can begin to misinterpret His motives simply because of poor communication.

If we are only temporary with the Word of God, we will not be equipped with the truth that silences the voice of the liar.

We then will begin to misinterpret the afflictions of Satan as afflictions of God. I pray for many people that credit the work of Satan to God. This mainly comes from the view that God controls everything that happens to us. With this view, we will believe that our circumstances—no matter how bad—must be part of God's plan. Without realizing it, we will find ourselves embracing an enemy we should be resisting.

Satan understands that the Word of God is designed to destroy his works. Affliction or persecution arises because of the Word sown in us. If we don't realize that the Word of God sown in us carries its own power to accomplish its purpose in our lives, we will find ourselves fighting against the Word designed for victory by crediting the work of Satan to God.

Time and again, people come to me for prayer, saying something like this: "God is allowing all this affliction in my life to teach me a lesson." You may be facing suffering and affliction in your life, but it is a byproduct of warfare against believers, not God's will. The Word of God initiates warfare because it represents a threat to Satan. Let's look at what Scripture has to say about affliction and persecution and your response to it.

Second Timothy 3:12 clearly says that all who desire to live a godly life in Christ will suffer persecution. Why is this so? Warfare comes against believers because the godly values we are called to live and represent challenge satanic powers and principalities. Ephesians 3:10 says that we are here to reveal the manifold wisdom of God to the powers

> You may be facing suffering and affliction in your life, but it is a byproduct of warfare against believers, not God's will.

and principalities. We are placed on this earth to reshape it according to God's will; therefore, we should not be surprised when persecution happens.

Jesus never said we would not suffer in this life. He did say that through Him, we have the victory (see 1 Corinthians 15:57). As the people of God, we must not redefine the nature of godliness to avoid persecution or to fit into culture. You and I are here as God's covenant people to hold the world accountable to the standard of God. We must be careful not to credit the work of the devil to God.

Responding to Persecution

Scripture tells us to love our enemies and pray for those who persecute us (see Matthew 5:44). This godly posture is so important because Satan likes to attack us through people so that we dehumanize them. If Satan can change the way you view someone, he can use your voice to bring death instead of life (see Proverbs 18:21). Part of our vocation as believers is reconciling people back to God (see 2 Corinthians 5:19–20). But how can we reconcile people back to God if we do not view them the way He views them? The heart of reconciliation based on 2 Corinthians 5 is not counting others' trespasses against them.

We must not see people as they are, but as they were created to be. Each one of us was formed in the image of God for the purpose of being an exact representation of Him on earth. We are to call people back to that original design. However, if we allow Satan to change this view, then we allow him to change the message God has given us. We need to be aware of these tactics and realize that our fight is not against enemies of flesh and blood but against satanic powers and principalities (see Ephesians 6:12).

Another way we are called to respond to persecution is to bless—not curse—those who persecute us (see Romans 12:14). Think about this for a moment. If you fight accusation with accusation, the only thing that wins is accusation. If you fight evil with evil, the only thing that wins is evil. Satan tempts us by projecting himself upon us, hoping that we come into agreement with him. If Satan can get us to mirror his attacks, we escalate evil on earth.

I once bumped into this warlock that began to speak curses over me. When this first started happening, I didn't respond like a Christian but responded in anger, hatred, and accusation. This went on for several months before I realized that I had fallen into a trap of Satan. Once I realized my mistake and understood that the person wasn't my enemy, the situation changed. He didn't realize what he was doing because he was taken over by the demonic. The enemy was Satan operating in this man. With that realization, I was able to see him through the eyes of Christ. This shift in perspective allowed me to start praying for his salvation instead of partnering with his destruction. Let me say it again—Satan's strategy is for us to mirror his attacks to escalate his purposes on earth.

> Satan's strategy is for us to mirror his attacks to escalate his purposes on earth.

We need to have a certain heart posture, especially in times of persecution, that is found in 2 Corinthians 12. In this passage, Paul talks about being tormented by a messenger of Satan.

Because of the extraordinary greatness of the revelations, for this reason, to keep me from exalting myself, there was given me a thorn in the flesh, a messenger of Satan to torment me—to keep me from exalting myself!

v. 7

Notice that Satan—not God—is afflicting Paul. What is Paul's response? What is his posture in the midst of this suffering?

Concerning this I pleaded with the Lord three times that it might leave me. And He has said to me, "My grace is sufficient for you, for power is perfected in weakness." Most gladly, therefore, I will rather boast about my weaknesses, so that the power of Christ may dwell in me. Therefore I delight in weaknesses, in insults, in distresses, in persecutions, in difficulties, in behalf of Christ; for when I am weak, then I am strong.

vv. 8–10

Paul is fully content with weaknesses, insults, distresses, persecutions, and difficulties for Christ's sake. We need this same heart posture if we are going to prevail in the time of evil. I am not saying that you will experience affliction or that you have to experience it. I'm simply highlighting what we tend to ignore in Scripture.

To relate this back to the parable of the seed in Matthew, Paul was not "temporary with the Word." In other words, he was internally controlled by the Word so that his relationship with Christ was not altered by circumstances. He was relationally involved with Christ daily so that when times of affliction came upon him, he didn't fall away or demonize the motives of God by crediting what was, in fact, the work of Satan to God.

Paul understood that believers will experience affliction and that God will sustain us, particularly in our weakness, which perfects His power. God is always seeking for us to partner our will with His will so that His will can be accomplished both in our lives and in the world. God causes the growth of the seed, and we maintain the conditions of our soil, which are our hearts.

How Satan Chokes Out the Word

Now, let's turn our attention to Luke 8:14: "The seed which fell among the thorns, these are the ones who have heard, and as they go on their way they are choked by worries, riches, and pleasures of this life, and they bring no fruit to maturity." I want to unpack three aspects of this verse that address how Satan chokes out the Word of God: worry, riches, and the pleasures of life. We need to look at these through the Word of God if we are to be a fruitful people. We will look at worry in the rest of this chapter and examine riches and the pleasures of life in the next chapter.

Worry

Scripture very specifically tells us how to handle worry.

> Do not be anxious about anything, but in everything by prayer and pleading with thanksgiving let your requests be made known to God. And the peace of God, which surpasses all comprehension, will guard your hearts and minds in Christ Jesus.
>
> Philippians 4:6–7

I have returned to these verses many times in my Christian journey because of all the truth packed into them. First, we are to be anxious for nothing. Yet if you look around, most people seem to operate in just the opposite way and are anxious about everything. Anxiety and worry go hand in hand. They are two sides of the same coin. This text tells us that we control worry in our lives.

With that said, most of the time, worries come from improper thinking or an improper use of the imagination, such as worrying about something that isn't real or that will probably never happen. When I was a kid, I loved to sit on the porch and play video games. Sometimes I would lose track of time and be out there for several hours. One day, I spent all afternoon playing on the front porch while my mom was in the house, worrying that I had been across the street with the druggies.

> Worries come from improper thinking or an improper use of imagination, such as worrying about something that isn't real or that will probably never happen.

I walked into the house, and before I could make it to my room, my mom said, "I know you've been across the street with those druggies." Even though I told her I had been sitting on the porch all afternoon, she wouldn't listen. Her worry was a result of improper thinking. What she was worried about all afternoon wasn't even real. Her imagination led her down a path of worry that produced a false impression. Worriers can take anything in life and stress about it until the imagination makes it worse than it really is. If you lead your emotions through unnecessary trauma often enough, you might find yourself living in an emotional prison.

So how do we stay off shaky emotional ground? According to Philippians 4:6, we are to go to the Lord in everything. However, many people live as if the verse says, "Go to the Lord when you are in trouble." Of course, we are to go to the Lord when we are in trouble, but if that is the only time we go to the Lord in prayer, then our relationship with God is based on crisis. Another way to put it would be to say that we need a crisis to have a relationship with Christ. When crisis becomes the basis of our relationship with God, then our relationship is external not internal. God is not far off in the sky somewhere. He is abiding inside us as His temple (see 1 Corinthians 3:16).

Prayer is about a relationship with the God that abides within, not about the demands we make of God. He is not a genie in a bottle that we awaken when we need Him and then put back when we don't. You probably have someone in your life who only comes around when they need something. How do you feel when you see their phone number on the caller ID? Does God feel the same way when He sees your prayer requests? Thankfully, the answer is no, but I think you get my point here. When you go to the Lord in everything, you will be prepared for all things.

Come with Thanksgiving

As we saw in Philippians 4:6, Scripture says that we are to come with thanksgiving when we approach God in prayer. Sadly, too many people act as if this verse says to come to Him with complaining. Complaining doesn't celebrate the presence of God but celebrates the presence of Satan. Complaining is using your voice to worship Satan. In the same way you enter God's gates with thanksgiving (see Psalm 100:4), you will enter Satan's gates with complaining. Complaining sends a signal in the spirit realm to all the demons in the neighborhood to come over to your house to be worshipped. When they arrive, your complaining will become supernaturally and demonically empowered. At that point, you will feel compelled to complain because it's demonically driven. People that complain a lot will always have drama in their lives simply because they create an atmosphere for demonic activity to thrive.

If you struggle to find something to be thankful for, I encourage you right now to take a moment and think back over your history with God. Instead of looking for all the bad things that have happened to you, look for those moments of happiness, breakthrough, joy, peace, healing, or other blessings. Once you find those positive memories, use them as a springboard so you can approach God in a thankful state of mind.

Often, our state of mind determines our level of thankfulness. I have learned over the years to celebrate all the things that have gone my way in life instead of focusing on all the bad. When you do this, it becomes easier to remain thankful in the midst of every circumstance. Thankfulness enables you to develop a victorious mindset in spite of what is happening around you.

The peace of God is to guard and protect our minds from the worry of this world based on human reasoning. When I approach God from a place of thankfulness, I end up in the place of peace described in Philippians 4:7. "And the peace of God, which surpasses all comprehension, will guard your hearts and minds in Christ Jesus." In fact, I have been in situations where the peace of God in my life has shocked people—people who were trying to put worry, fear, and depression on me because that is how they were responding to the situation. The peace of

God will not make sense to an unbeliever; it cannot be understood according to the logic of this world. So we must not allow the opinions of man to become the voice of reason. God has put us here to reveal Him to the world. If we, as God's people, respond no differently than unbelievers, what kind of message does that send to those that need hope?

Let's look at one more passage from the Gospel of Matthew that addresses the issue of worry.

For this reason I say to you, do not be worried about your life, as to what you will eat or what you will drink; nor for your body, as to what you will put on. Is life not more than food, and the body more than clothing? Look at the birds of the sky, that they do not sow, nor reap, nor gather crops into barns, and yet your heavenly Father feeds them. Are you not much more important than they? And which of you by worrying can add a single day to his life's span? And why are you worried about clothing? Notice how the lilies of the field grow; they do not labor nor do they spin thread for cloth, yet I say to you that not even Solomon in all his glory clothed himself like one of these. But if God so clothes the grass of the field, which is alive today and tomorrow is thrown into the furnace, will He not much more clothe you? You of little faith! Do not worry then, saying, "What are we to eat?" or "What are we to drink?" or "What are we to wear for clothing?" For the Gentiles eagerly seek all these things; for your heavenly Father knows that you need all these things. But seek first His kingdom and His righteousness, and all these things will be provided to you.

So do not worry about tomorrow; for tomorrow will worry about itself. Each day has enough trouble of its own.

Matthew 6:25–34

This passage begins with the statement "Do not be worried about your life." Scripture frequently tells us not to worry because God is very serious about the damage worry will do to us. This passage goes on to list common areas in life that we worry about, such as our need for food and clothing. Satan is also looking at these areas and evaluating how we respond to these daily needs. The passage continues by connecting the common needs to the ways in which God meets those needs. God then asks an important rhetorical question: "Are you not worth more than [the birds and the flowers]?" He wants us to understand that we are extremely valuable in His eyes. We are the crown of His creation. If He is willing to meet the needs of the flowers in the fields, how much more will He meet the needs of His people?

> We maintain faith by shifting our attention from seeking daily needs to seeking the kingdom.

God follows this question by connecting it to faith. Faith is how we receive from the kingdom of God. Everything in His kingdom is received by faith. So if faith receives, then unbelief rejects. The question then becomes, "How do I maintain faith?"

The last part of these verses gives us the answer—we maintain faith by shifting our attention from seeking daily needs to seeking the kingdom. As we shift our attention, our faith becomes anchored not in daily needs but in the faithfulness of God. We should never become so preoccupied with daily needs that we fail to see God's faithfulness surrounding us. No matter what troubles and worries come our way, God's faithfulness provides all that we need to live a victorious life.

Prayer

Lord Jesus, I call upon your grace to live according to truth. I prepare my heart for the incorruptible seed of your Word to be planted. Jesus, I dedicate my life to the planting and reaping of the Word through me. I choose to embrace the process, in Jesus's name!

Weapons for the Battle

1. To maintain a victorious mindset during suffering and trials, remember you have the authority to determine your internal experience. Your state of being is dependent upon the mediation of your mind. You may not be able to control what happens *to* you, but you can control what happens *in* you. The Holy Spirit is abiding inside you. As you renew your mind to that reality, you will begin to experience the fruit of the Spirit within you.

2. The truth of the Word is your weapon of warfare. Don't just talk to God about your circumstances, also talk to your circumstances about God. Use the Word to speak to the mountain to be removed. If you're sick, find Scriptures about healing to speak to it. If you're in financial crisis, use Bible verses that remind you that God is your provider to speak to it. In other words, speak back to what speaks to you. Find at least five specific Bible references that apply to your mountain: marriage, children, work, finances, health, etc. Memorize

the verses. Write them out on notecards to put up notecards in strategic spots: in your car, on the bathroom
mirror, on the fridge, etc. Claim your victory!

3. Use gratitude as a weapon by reflecting on your history with God and thanking Him for times of comfort
and victory. Keep a gratitude journal for thirty days.
List three things a day that you are thankful for. Who
knows? You might even want to continue after the
thirty days.

4. If you find yourself getting caught up in the little distractions of life, shift your attention from seeking daily
needs to perceiving what God is doing and asking "on
earth as it is in heaven."

6

ENTANGLED IN THE TEMPORARY

Eternity is a fascinating concept. However, most people do not live their lives with eternity in mind. In fact, most people only think in relation to their lives in this world. We spend all of our time working to build a natural kingdom that we will not be able to take into eternity with us. First, there is absolutely nothing wrong with working to make a better life for yourself now. That is not what I'm addressing here. I'm simply stating the fact that most of the time, we do not think from eternity's perspective. What if we did? How would it impact our priorities and the way we spent our time now?

When I first started thinking from eternity's perspective, I was a youth pastor, primarily of kids from broken homes. Many of the parents didn't seem to make much time for their children. They were either preoccupied with their own career or their own agendas. This grieved my heart for the youth.

All they wanted was to see someone supporting them at their games, plays, projects, and so forth. Even though I was a youth pastor, I also worked two other jobs. However, I made a commitment to these kids to be there for them. I wanted them to look up from their activities and see someone cheering them on. As I started attending their events, I realized that what I thought was important was not that big of a deal. Then it dawned on me that what matters most from eternity's perspective are the people in our lives and the time we have to spend with them. I saw that what I thought were important things were simply temporal realties that will one day fade.

Let's keep this in mind as we focus on the third aspect of Luke 8:14. The Gospel of Matthew tells us how we should posture our hearts in regard to riches.

> Do not store up for yourselves treasures on earth, where moth and rust destroy, and where thieves break in and steal. But store up for yourselves treasures in heaven, where neither moth nor rust destroys, and where thieves do not break in or steal; for where your treasure is, there your heart will be also.
>
> Matthew 6:19–21

This powerful passage gives us the heart posture necessary for the fruit of the kingdom to be produced in a person's life. Riches can seriously hinder the growth of the kingdom. Riches in themselves are not evil; however, if we do not hold them in proper perspective, they will have a strong grip on our hearts. As verse 21 says, "For where your treasure is, there your heart will be also." In other words, what the heart celebrates, it also treasures.

God wants to set our priorities in life in His eternal perspective, not the temporal. We become preoccupied with space, time, and the material world, and those become our priorities. How different would your life be if you viewed it from God's eternal perspective? How would that change your priorities? Look around, and you will see so many who are conformed to this world in today's culture. We are not called to be conformed to this world (see Romans 12:2), so therefore, we shouldn't view life only within the context of this world. Satan wants us to conform and shift us to his priorities, and he does that by distracting us from the reality of heaven. There is nothing wrong with riches and possessions in themselves. The question is, "Do you have riches, or do riches have you?" Your answer will reveal what your heart treasures.

> There is nothing wrong with riches and possessions in themselves. The question is, "Do you have riches, or do riches have you?" Your answer will reveal what your heart treasures.

Let's look at the story of the rich young ruler.

And someone came to Him and said, "Teacher, what good thing shall I do so that I may obtain eternal life?" And He said to him, "Why are you asking Me about what is good? There is only One who is good; but if you want to enter life, keep the commandments." Then he said to Him, "Which ones?" And Jesus said, "You shall not commit murder; you shall not commit adultery; you shall not steal; you shall not give false testimony; honor your father and mother; and you shall love your neighbor as yourself." The young man said to Him, "All these I have kept; what am I still lacking?" Jesus said to him, "If you want to be complete, go and sell your possessions and give to the poor, and you will have treasure in heaven; and come, follow Me." But when the young man heard this statement, he went away grieving; for he was one who owned much property.

Matthew 19:16–22

Interestingly, this rich young man wanted only to do the minimum necessary for eternal life and nothing more. This seems to be a predominant line of thought in today's culture. People generally only want to give up the minimum amount to consider Christ as their Lord. In many ways, we want to be just obedient enough to feel comfortable with our disobedience. People want to feel as if Jesus is Lord of their lives while not actually letting Him be their Lord. Jesus knew the major heart issue of the rich young ruler, and so He told him to sell all his possessions and give to the poor.

Now, this wasn't because Jesus wanted him to live in poverty. He knew the real obstacle in this man's life was his riches. His possessions were his provider, not God. Sadly, the man was not able to let go of his worldly possessions. Anything we are not willing to give up is an idol of worship that needs to be sacrificed. God is our one and only provider. Many struggle with this same stumbling block, and sadly, many respond as the rich young ruler did.

Pleasures of Life

What does Scripture mean when it talks about the "pleasures of life?" Second Timothy has the answer.

But realize this, that in the last days difficult times will come. For people will be lovers of self, lovers of money, boastful, arrogant, slanderers, disobedient to parents, ungrateful, unholy, unloving, irreconcilable, malicious gossips, without self-control, brutal, haters of good, treacherous, reckless, conceited, lovers of pleasure rather than lovers of God, holding to a form of godliness, although they have denied its power; avoid such people as these.

2 Timothy 3:1–5

In this passage, the people Paul is referring to are those who hold to a form of godliness but have denied its power. We are warned to stay away from such people. We should not brush off these strong statements. Scripture is warning us that this type of life deceives us into thinking we are someone we are not. This type of Christianity is what I refer to as "nominal Christianity." Nominal Christians are those who profess Christ by name but live for themselves in principle. Satan loves to see us fall into the illusion we are serving God while, in reality, we are serving ourselves in His name. This was the same crossroads that the rich young ruler came to. Timothy is talking about those who live to fulfill the desires of self.

Satan loves nominal Christians because everything in their lives is shaped by his nature of self-centeredness. Self-centeredness was the root cause of Satan's fall (Isaiah 14:13–15) and is the root cause of nominal Christianity today. A nominal Christian lives oblivious to the lordship of Christ because that person only views themselves as the lord of their life. This type of thinking is destroying Christianity by disconnecting "Christ as Savior" from "Christ as Lord." Nominal Christians want the benefit of a Savior without any responsibility to Him as the God of their life.

My wife, Chantal Rose Wood, spent her childhood into her early adulthood as a nominal Christian. She professed Christ as Savior but had no context for Him as Lord until she had a radical encounter with His power and was delivered of suicide, depression, and lust. This took place one night after leaving a church service after a man shared his testimony of deliverance. Once she heard his story, she realized that she didn't know Christ in a relational way. She knew about Him as a Savior from her sins, but not as God in her daily life. As she was driving home, she cried out to the Lord with tears streaming down her face. "I understand now! I fully surrender my life to You. Wherever You want me to go, I will go. Whatever You want me to do, I will do."

As she prayed, the tangible presence of God came into her car with His waves of liquid love, and for the first time, she understood what it meant to be a born-again believer. You see, salvation is not just a confession but a conversion. Chantal pulled the car over as the power of God came upon her, and she was delivered of the demons that had been tormenting her. From that moment on, she knew Christ in a different way—no longer as a distant Savior but as a close personal God to be served. Scripture says you have been bought with a price so glorify God with your body (1 Corinthians 6:20). Jesus cannot be *a* lord in your life. He is to be *the* Lord of your life. Each person must choose.

> Jesus cannot be *a* lord in your life. He is to be *the* Lord of your life. Each person must choose.

For years, I was bound by addiction to drugs until I was set free by the audible voice of God at my salvation experience. Since that time, I have had many desires to drink, smoke, or party. The difference is that now, those desires are subject to the Spirit of God within me. Now I'm the one in the driver's seat because of the power of the Spirit. Romans 8:6 clarifies this when it says, "For the mind set on the flesh is death, but the mind set on the Spirit is life and peace." God wants us to understand that our mindset determines which desires we resist or empower. Paul, in his letter to the Galatians, lays this out very clearly.

> But I say, walk by the Spirit, and you will not carry out the desire of the flesh. For the desire of the flesh is against the Spirit, and the Spirit against the flesh; for these are in opposition to one another, in order to keep you from doing whatever you want. But if you are led by the Spirit, you are not under the Law. Now the deeds of the flesh are evident, which are: sexual immorality, impurity, indecent behavior, idolatry, witchcraft, hostilities, strife, jealousy, outbursts of anger, selfish ambition, dissensions, factions, envy, drunkenness, carousing, and things like these, of which I forewarn you, just as I have forewarned you, that those who practice such things will not inherit the kingdom of God.
>
> Galatians 5:16–21

Paul's line of thought in this passage is extraordinarily profound and enlightening. The first two verses clearly lay out the contrast that every believer will experience—the flesh sets its desires against the spirit, and the spirit sets its desires against the flesh. You might say, "Wait a minute! Aren't we each a new creation liberated from the desires of the flesh?" Yes, but only if we walk by the Spirit of God. Liberation doesn't mean you are no longer susceptible to the desires of the flesh. It means you are no longer captive to its power. In other words, you can now resist the desires you were once controlled by, and that's good news.

Consider what Paul says in 1 Corinthians 9:27: "But I strictly discipline my body and make it my slave, so that, after I have preached to others, I myself will not be disqualified." If Paul was already liberated from the desires of the flesh, why would he still need to bring it into submission? Because Paul wasn't liberated from the desire itself; he was liberated from the desire's control over him. He no longer had to obey the desire. The desires of his flesh had to obey him. The power to live free is the liberation of the Spirit.

If this is still hard for you to consider, think about it from another angle. If God fully liberated you from desire itself, He would have stripped you of a free will. C. S. Lewis once said, "Free will, though it makes evil possible, is also the only thing that makes possible any love or goodness or joy worth having."[1] God is not going to violate the most precious gift He has given us, which is our will.

If you didn't have a will, it would be impossible for you to live in disobedience to God. This would mean that God had total control over you. The reality is that God is not seeking to control you but to liberate you. If God wanted to control us, He would not have given us a will. God gave us a will so that we can choose to submit to Him. Fleshly desires will always be there, but when we are in Christ, we get to choose whether to submit to those fleshly desires.

As we come to the close of this parable, you can see the first three types of soil did not produce the fruit intended. You will also notice that the same seed was cast on all the different types of soil, which means every soil contained the same potential harvest.

> But the seed in the good soil, these are the ones who have heard the word with a good and virtuous heart, and hold it firmly, and produce fruit with perseverance.
>
> Luke 8:15

1. C. S. Lewis, *Mere Christianity* (New York: Simon & Schuster, 1996), 52–53.

Notice here that the seed that was sown needed compatible soil in order to yield the harvest God intended, meaning that God is responsible for the growth of the seed while we are responsible for the condition of our soil. It's not one or the other but the combination of the two—seed and soil—that results in the harvest.

For example, my wife had a dream where she was in a nearby city. She was walking down a street where merchants were selling merchandise on the sidewalks. One of the merchants had this beautiful pair of blue shoes that she wanted. So she ran over to the merchant and stole the blue shoes. She then woke from the dream with the Spirit of the Lord hovering over her, speaking a *rhema* word to her. "Stop letting the devil steal the revelation you have on healing," the Lord said.

She replied, "Oh no, I didn't realize I was doing that, Lord! I repent for doing that. Please, Father, help me remember in the moment when I need to partner with your healing truth."

> God is responsible for the growth of the seed while we are responsible for the condition of our soil. It's not one or the other but the combination of the two—seed and soil—that results in the harvest.

Shortly after this experience, she was hurrying to get to work one morning. As she stepped out the door, she twisted her ankle. Her first thought was, "Now I have to call in sick to work today." But as she paused and said no to that thought, the Lord spoke to her about His healing. She immediately started walking on her injured foot while commanding her foot to be healed and to line up with Scripture. By the time she got to her car over two blocks away, her foot was healed.

The fruit we bear reveals the allegiance we have either to God or Satan. Partnership with God is necessary for His kingdom to bear fruit in our lives. In the same way, Satan is seeking our partnership to produce the reality of his corrupt and evil kingdom in our lives. Again, I want to remind you that we each get to choose who we submit to.

This is misunderstood in the body of Christ. The reality is God has His part, and we have our part in fulfilling His will. You can even say it this way: God is seeking the partnership of our wills so that His can be accomplished. That doesn't mean that God cannot do things without us. However, it does mean that we as His body are His primary avenue in moving on the earth today. Consider this passage:

> But now I am going to Him who sent Me; and none of you asks Me, 'Where are You going?' But because I have said these things to you, grief has filled your heart. But I tell you the truth: it is to your advantage that I am leaving; for if I do not leave, the Helper will not come to you; but if I go, I will send Him to you. And He, when He comes, will convict the world regarding sin, and righteousness, and judgment: regarding sin, because they do not believe in Me; and regarding righteousness, because I am going to the Father and you no longer are going to see Me; and regarding judgment, because the ruler of this world has been judged.
>
> John 16:5–11

In this passage of Scripture, Jesus is speaking to His disciples about a coming helper. What is amazing about these texts is the emphasis Jesus places on His coming. First, let me give context to these statements. Jesus is about to go to the cross to be crucified. He is explaining some very powerful truths to the disciples before His departure. One of these truths is that it will be better for them that He leaves. My first thought would be, *What is better than having Jesus in the flesh?* The disciples can see Jesus. They can touch Him. They can hear Him and smell Him. Jesus is walking among them in His flesh, helping them through life. So what is better than that?

According to Jesus, having Him by the Spirit is better for us than having Him in His physical form. Jesus is trying to get the disciples to understand that it is actually to their advantage that He come to them in a different form. You and I live in the time that Jesus was speaking about to the disciples. We live in the time of a greater advantage because we have the indwelling presence of Christ abiding within us by His Spirit.

As you read through these texts, Jesus says that the Spirit comes as a helper. That helper is seeking partnership or agreement of our will. Jesus didn't send the Spirit as our servant but as our helper to come alongside us. God has His part, and we have our part. In order for us to walk in the victory and the freedom Christ died for, we must learn to take advantage of the indwelling presence of Christ. So how do we become sensitive to God? How do we become the good soil? Let's reflect on the parable we have been studying to see.

Good Soil

We have looked at what happens to the seed of God when it falls beside the road or in a rocky, thorny place. But what about the seed that falls on good soil? What happens to that seed? "And others fell on the good soil and yielded a crop, some a hundred, some sixty, and some thirty times as much" (Matthew 13:8).

The "good soil" here is the heart posture necessary to reap the harvest of our potential. The person with an honest and good heart that holds to the Word of God with perseverance is good soil. John 15 tells us what it means to prepare our heart to be good soil by abiding and pruning:

> I am the true vine, and My Father is the vinedresser. Every branch in Me that does not bear fruit, He takes away; and every branch that bears fruit, He prunes it so that it may bear more fruit. You are already clean because of the word which I have spoken to you. Remain in Me, and I in you. Just as the branch cannot bear fruit of itself but must remain in the vine, so neither can you unless you remain in Me. I am the vine, you are the branches; the one who remains in me, and I in him, bears much fruit, for apart from Me you can do nothing. If anyone does not remain in Me, he is thrown away like a branch and dries up; and they gather them and throw them into the fire and they are burned. If you remain in Me, and My words remain in you, ask whatever you wish, and it will be done for you. My Father is glorified by this, that you bear much fruit, and so prove to be My disciples. Just as the Father has loved Me, I also have loved you; remain in My love. If you keep My commandments, you will remain in My love; just as I have kept My Father's commandments and remain in His love. These things I have spoken to you so that My joy may be in you, and that your joy may be made full.
>
> John 15:1–11

In order to fully receive the rich revelation in this passage, let's break it down verse by verse.

Abiding in Christ, the Vine

> I am the true vine, and My Father is the vinedresser. Every branch in Me that does not bear fruit, He takes away; and every branch that bears fruit, He prunes it so that it may bear more fruit.
>
> John 15:1–2

These two verses lay out the context for everything mentioned after this point. They make a clear and definitive statement that Jesus is the vine and the Father is the vinedresser. What does this mean? As "the vine," Jesus is the one we find our true identity in. First Corinthians 6:17 says that the one who has joined himself to the Lord has become one spirit with Him. The word *one* means "singular"—we are in total and complete union with Christ. There is never a moment of separation from Him (see Hebrews 13:5) "because as He is, we also are in this world" (1 John 4:17). So the only way we don't abide is if we live ignorant of our union, our oneness with Christ. Abiding in Christ, who is the vine, is the heart posture we need.

God Is the Vinedresser

Second, we are to allow the Father to prune us. Father God tends to the branches; the branches do not tend to themselves. Remember this vital point in order to bear the fruit intended for your life. God has to be the one pruning because He knows how to prune your life to enable you to produce the necessary growth.

We should never position ourselves to be the vinedresser. When we do, we are trying to put ourselves in the position of God. We are trying to be our own Savior. Introspection becomes the counterfeit to the role of God in our lives. When we try to prune ourselves, we stunt our growth, which results in barrenness in a season God intended for fruitfulness. When we allow Father God to prune us, He will do it in a way that causes growth without doing damage.

I went through a two-year period in my own life regarding my natural father. At the time, I heard some teaching stating that we generally tend to project our own wounds with our natural father onto God. However, this is true only if we engage in that kind of projection. In my situation, I honestly never projected those things onto God. I never once looked at God through the lens of my natural father. This wasn't an issue in my life until I heard teaching that took me into a period of introspection that had me looking for an issue that wasn't there. My father wounds had already been dealt with and healed, but when I started circling back around to them through my own urging, I went through a period of confusion. If God has dealt with something in your heart, leave it alone unless He brings it up again.

Sanctification

Now, let's look at what John has to say about sanctification.

> You are already clean because of the word which I have spoken to you. Abide in Me, and I in you. As the branch cannot bear fruit of itself unless it abides in the vine, so neither can you unless you abide in Me.
>
> John 15:3–4 NASB95

As I'm sure you have discovered by now, there is a difference between getting free and staying free. Verse 3 gives insight into how that is reconciled while verse 4 seals the deal with the statement "abide in me" because the branch cannot bear fruit of itself. We must abide. A moment of freedom is not the same as a lifestyle of freedom unless we remain faithful to abide in the vine. The Word of God spoken over us has already sanctified us (John 17:17). You just need to remember that the Word that sanctified you in the past is also the same Word that will keep you sanctified in the present.

When I was an alcoholic, I went through several attempts to kick that addiction. I made a very sincere choice and effort that my drinking days were over. Several times, I even made it a week or two without any cravings. I got into this place of victory and thought, *It's over! I have kicked the habit!*

Once that feeling of victory came over me, I wanted to celebrate, so naturally, I called the only people I knew—fellow alcoholics. They were my friends, and it wouldn't hurt to just hang out with them. But I didn't realize that I was walking right back into bondage. Every time I spent time with those drinking buddies, I found myself drinking before the night was over.

As believers, we make this common mistake all the time. We have a divine encounter and think our issues are done, taken care of forever. Then, as we gradually become familiar with our newfound freedom, we drift from relationship with the Lord until we disconnect ourselves from the vine that keeps us free. There is no freedom for those disconnected from the vine that is Jesus. Period. John lays it out clearly.

> I am the vine, you are the branches; he who abides in Me and I in him, he bears much fruit, for apart from Me you can do nothing. If anyone does not abide in Me, he is thrown away as

a branch and dries up; and they gather them, and cast them into the fire and they are burned.

John 15:5–6 NASB95

Verse 5 reemphasizes the importance of abiding in Christ. Consider it this way: Romans 12:1 declares that we are to be a living sacrifice, which is our spiritual service of worship to Christ. As a living sacrifice, we have to choose daily to remain on the altar, choose daily to remain in Christ. This kind of living brings us to the hard reality of verse 6. Anyone that does not remain in Christ will be thrown away. Let's be clear here: Jesus is not the one who throws people away. Our willful rejection of abiding in Christ gets us thrown away. I find this very sobering, and I hope you do too.

The major way we disconnect and become unfruitful is by separating ourselves from Christ in our minds. You can be in total union with Christ in spirit but alienated from God in your mind. If Christ is abiding inside us, He is there as our helper. We yield to His help by renewing our minds according to the Word. Ultimately, what we are doing is bringing our will under submission to His. Renewing the mind is not being introspective but displacing lies with the truth of God's Word. So again, Matthew 15:8 says, "These people honor me with their lips, but their hearts are far from me" (NIV). The heart includes the mind, so the thoughts and intentions of the heart are the things that are most important to God (see 1 Samuel 16:7).

Abiding in His Word

If you abide in Me, and My words abide in you, ask whatever you wish, and it will be done for you. My Father is glorified

by this, that you bear much fruit, and so prove to be My
disciples.

John 15:7–8 NASB95

These two verses are powerful when we really grasp what is
being communicated. Verse 7 sets another tone regarding what
abiding in Christ consists of. We abide in Christ and allow His
Word to abide in us. Based on this passage, when we allow
His Word to abide in us, we can ask whatever we desire. We
could easily think this is an exaggeration and disregard this
passage; however, we need to consider what is being said. Look
at what Jesus was communicating in John 8:

> So Jesus was saying to those Jews who had believed Him, "If
> you continue in My word, then you are truly My disciples; and
> you will know the truth, and the truth will set you free."

John 8:31–32

These verses echo what Jesus said in John 15:8. We prove to be
His disciples by continuing *in His Word* (my emphasis). Jesus
makes this statement and then tells the disciples that the fruit
they will experience when they continue in His Word is "ultimate freedom." As you see in this context, only the disciples
that remain faithful to His Word walk in freedom. Likewise,
when we remain faithful to abiding in Christ and live in obedience to His Word, we can ask whatever we wish because His
desires and our desires are the same.

Maybe this is what God meant in Psalm 37:4. "Delight yourself in the LORD; and He will give you the desires of your heart."
I'm sure we have all prayed for something and then didn't see
the fruit of that prayer. Maybe we are not praying according

111

to His desires but according to our desires independent of His Word.

One of my favorite things to do when I get up in the morning is to spend the first two hours of my day studying the Word of God. Since I've been doing this, my day is fruitful, and I'm not constantly battling against thoughts in my mind because my mind is stayed upon the Lord (see Isaiah 26:3). Often, when I think about something I want, God will actually bless me with that very thing for no particular reason other than because He loves me and loves that I abide in Him.

For example, I wanted to buy an Apple watch, but my wife kept telling me not to spend so much money on a watch. Like a good husband, I listened to my wife. A little while later, when I was in San Diego doing a conference, a gentleman walked up and gave me an Apple watch. All I could think about at that moment was the delight of my heavenly Father over me.

Showing Your Love for God

Just as the Father has loved Me, I also have loved you; remain in My love. If you keep My commandments, you will remain in My love; just as I have kept My Father's commandments and remain in His love. These things I have spoken to you so that My joy may be in you, and that your joy may be made full.

John 15:9–11

In these verses, Jesus gives us some powerful truths to consider. First, when we keep Father God's commandments, it is a sign of our love for Him. Your relationship with the Father can be compared to any intimate relationship you have. When you're in an intimate relationship with someone, you find yourself doing things that you normally would not do simply because you are looking for ways to show your love for the person. For example, you do some things for your spouse, children, or family members not because you have to but because you love them.

I like to go outside and ride, walk, or spend time outdoors. My wife is an inside person. She would much rather be in the house, wrapped up in a blanket on the sofa. However, she will spend time outside with me simply because she loves me. Whenever she does this, it blesses me so much because I know she is sacrificing for me. Things done in love are not chores or laws you must maintain. Instead, they are your way to show love. When you approach the commandments of God in the same way, it shifts the way you view them altogether. Obeying God's commandments becomes an opportunity to show your love for Him, not a chore to be completed.

The Joy of the Lord

A second thing you will notice in verses 9 to 11 is that Jesus gives us a promise that His joy will be in us to bring about the completion of our joy. Nehemiah said it this way: "Then he said to them, 'Go, eat the festival foods, drink the sweet drinks, and send portions to him who has nothing prepared; for this day is holy to our Lord. Do not be grieved, for the joy of the LORD is your refuge'" (Nehemiah 8:10).

Joy is a sign we are living in the strength of God. When we learn to fully abide in Christ and allow Father God to prune us, we begin to see the fruit of the kingdom produced in our lives. As the fruit of the kingdom begins to produce in us, we notice that what we ask for is being fulfilled because we find our desires in direct alignment with Father God, making them a delight that leaves us in a place of joy.

PRAYER

Father God, I pray that Your truths examined here will strengthen my walk and help me identify the tactics of Satan that are coming against the growth of Your kingdom in my life. May Your truths also help me identify any conditions of my heart that are hindering the growth of Your kingdom so that I might properly posture my heart to allow Your kingdom to fully produce Your intended purpose. In Jesus's name. Amen.

WEAPONS FOR THE BATTLE

1. Ask God to prune you so that what is good will bear even more fruit and what is bad will be cut off so that you can experience even greater joy. See Galatians 5:16–26 for what to cut off and what to add.

2. Make Jesus the Lord of your life, not just another source of information you listen to. Pray the following prayer if you haven't already. *Dear Jesus, You have been my Savior, and I have followed You when it was convenient. Please forgive me. I now make You Lord and King of my life. Rule and reign in my heart from this day forward, making my desires Your own. In Jesus's name. Amen.*

3. Abiding in Christ does not come by performance but by resting in His grace. If you are looking for a place to start, take thirty minutes of your morning and break it up into three eight-minute segments. First, worship the Lord with thanksgiving. This will prepare the heart for planting of the Word of God. Second, plant the seed of God's Word in your heart. You can find many reading plans to help you, including the plan on the YouVersion Bible app that goes with this book. The most important thing is creating the habit of study. Third, pray in the Spirit. When I pray in the Spirit after I study, revelation begins to flow to the mind. The Spirit will quicken the Word inside you. Fourth, take five or six minutes to meditate on what the Lord has quickened to you. Sit in a place of quietness and ponder the Scriptures. It helps me to picture myself in the storyline of Scripture. It makes it personal.

PART 2

GODLY WEAPONS TO FIGHT SATAN

7

THE VICTORY OF THE CROSS

The first part of this book was primarily aimed at exposing the tactics and schemes of Satan along with providing practical weapons for the battle when dealing with those issues. In the second part, we will be focusing on identifying more tools and weapons God has given us so that we can stand against the plans and schemes of the devil. My hope is to arm you with a fresh context for viewing Satan and his hosts of wickedness—to see him through the lens of Jesus and the victory of the cross. My aim is to show just how defeated Satan is in relation to you as a Christian. He is not some overwhelming, powerful being you have to tolerate. He is a defeated, disarmed foe when compared to Christ.

As we dive into this next section, I pray that you will begin to view yourself differently as well. I pray that your self-image will be as someone hidden in Christ. You are a victor, not a victim! With that being said, let's look at Ephesians 6 and identify the weapons of your warfare. Everything you need to know about spiritual warfare stems from the understanding of the armor of God. As we look at the armor of God, this will help us learn to walk in victory, not just to occasionally experience it.

> Put on the full armor of God, so that you will be able to stand firm against the schemes of the devil. For our struggle is not against flesh and blood, but against the rulers, against the powers, against the world forces of this darkness, against the spiritual forces of wickedness in the heavenly places. Therefore, take up the full armor of God, so that you will be able to resist in the evil day, and having done everything, to stand firm. Stand firm therefore, having girded your loins with truth, and having put on the breastplate of righteousness, and having shod your feet with the preparation of the gospel of peace; in addition to all, taking up the shield of faith with which you will be able to extinguish all the flaming arrows of the evil one. And take the helmet of salvation, and the sword of the Spirit, which is the word of God. With all prayer and petition pray at all times in the Spirit, and with this in view, be on the alert with all perseverance and petition for all the saints.
>
> Ephesians 6:11–18 NASB95

In 2008, I had a three-month encounter with the Lord where He began to teach me about spiritual warfare. I began to see tremendous breakthrough in the area of deliverance and exercising the victory of the blood of Jesus over my city. In addition, I started experiencing personal wholeness in ways I never thought possible. Ephesians 6 became a foundational building block for me during that season.

As you read through this passage, you will notice many things. I will highlight three of them to keep at the forefront of your mind as we study this passage.

1. First, we are putting on the armor of God, not the armor of man. We especially need to remember this in times of battle. The armor of man is designed to fight earthly enemies. The armor of God is designed to fight spiritual enemies.

2. Second, we are responsible to apply the armor of God to our lives. God gives the supply, and we must use it for His purposes. God has always intended to work on earth through His covenant people. He is seeking the partnership of your will so that His will can be accomplished.

3. Third, we need to be aware of seven specific foundational truths listed in Ephesians 6. We will be focusing on these verses to see what the Lord reveals.

Seven Foundational Truths for Spiritual Warfare

Truth #1: "Put on the full armor of God, so that you will be able to stand firm against the schemes of the devil" (Ephesians 6:11).

This verse immediately makes two very important points. First, God is only responsible for giving the supply; we are responsible for using it for His purposes. Jesus Himself said so: "For I have come down from heaven, not to do My own will, but the will of Him who sent Me" (John 6:38). Jesus is our role model for how we are to fulfill the will of the Father. God will never force His will on anyone. He gives the supply, and we partner with Him through willing submission. In fact, we can have as much of God's will as we want. God has chosen to create us this way because He wants each one of us to be an interdependent extension of Him on earth. Notice I said interdependent extension *of* God, not independent *from* Him.

Second, we need to put on the full armor so that we can stand against Satan. This very revealing statement is often overlooked in the body of Christ. Many times, we want God to fight for us when, in fact, He wants to fight through us. I'm not saying God doesn't fight battles for us. But the primary way He fights battles is through us because He enjoys demonstrating His power through vessels Satan deems as weak. In essence, God is saying that He intends to continue to defeat Satan through people made in His image as part of Satan's punishment. Through us, God is baiting Satan into a battle he (Satan) has already lost. In order to be battle ready, though, we must start by putting on the full armor.

Truth #2: "For our struggle is not against flesh and blood, but against the rulers, against the powers, against the world forces of this darkness, against the spiritual forces of wickedness in the heavenly places" (Ephesians 6:12).

Verse 12 lists one thing we are not fighting against and four things we are fighting against. First, we are not fighting against flesh and blood. I made this point earlier in the book, but let's look at it again. One of the greatest tricks of Satan is to get us to demonize people. They are not our enemy. When we demonize people, we engage in the wrong battle. We are fighting evil forces of wickedness, not one another. We must grasp this major truth if we are going to walk in victory. We need to live with an awareness that other factors—the spirit realm—are involved when dealing with people. In fact, consider this passage that speaks of unbelievers.

And although you were dead in your offenses and sins, in which you formerly lived according to this world's present path, according to the ruler of the domain of the air, the ruler of the spirit that is now energizing the sons of disobedience, among whom all of us also formerly lived out our lives in the cravings of our flesh, indulging the desires of the flesh and the mind, and were by nature children of wrath even as the rest.

Ephesians 2:1–3 NET

This text begins by stating that we who are born again have been freed from the ruler of the power of the air, who is Satan. This passage goes on to describe how a demonic spirit is at work within unbelievers. The term "sons of disobedience" is describing the unbelievers in the world. This spirit is energizing their disobedience with cravings of the flesh. I know these are very strong words, but we need to keep this in mind while living in the world. We must learn to separate the person from the spirit that is at work within them, to realize that people are victims of Satan. They are waiting for the sons of the kingdom to set them free.

> People are not our enemy. When we demonize people, we engage in the wrong battle. We are fighting evil forces of wickedness, not one another.

This passage first impacted me in 2012 when my brother was brutally murdered by a drug addict. At that time, I had been witnessing to him about Christ. He would always call me "preacher boy." Even though I didn't feel that I was making an impact on him, after his death, his friends told me that he always bragged about how I turned my life around.

An extrovert that was always having fun, my brother made everyone around him laugh. He had a unique way of connecting with others. When he died so tragically, many emotions were running through my mind. My thoughts toward the person that murdered him were not godly. However, I forced myself to look past the person and at the real enemy in the situation. The real enemy was not the person that murdered my brother; the real enemy was Satan working through the person.

For Satan to use a person, they must cooperate with him. But he is still the master planner of evil. When I recognized the real enemy, I could see that even this person was also a victim of Satan just as my brother was a victim of their actions. If I condemned that person to hell, I would be acting no differently than Satan. Instead, I started praying for that person's salvation and for her to be set free from bondage to the devil. I don't know whether she ever got saved, but I refused to repay evil with evil. If you fight evil with evil, the only thing that wins is evil. We overcome evil with good (see Romans 12:21).

In the time of Jesus, the long-awaited hope and belief of the people of God was that the coming Messiah would overthrow all the natural kingdoms and rulers of the earth, thereby liberating God's people. Yet Jesus came not to overthrow earthly kingdoms but to overthrow the spiritual rulers and spiritual kingdoms. The people were expecting an earthly conquering king instead of a suffering servant. They didn't realize that Jesus disarmed the spiritual forces of wickedness through His death and resurrection, thereby freeing people from the power and control of those forces. Paul tells us some important aspects of what Jesus accomplished:

When you were dead in your transgressions and the uncircumcision of your flesh, He made you alive together with Him, having forgiven us all our transgressions, having canceled out the certificate of debt consisting of decrees against us, which was hostile to us; and He has taken it out of the way, having nailed it to the cross. When He had disarmed the rulers and authorities, He made a public display of them, having triumphed over them through Him.

Colossians 2:13–15 NASB95

These three verses tell us four specific ways Jesus disarmed the spiritual forces of wickedness. First, Jesus forgave all our transgressions. This vital truth that Jesus has already forgiven each one of us all of our transgressions—past, present, and future—will help us withstand Satan when he talks in our ears, trying to cause us to sin. By definition, "sin" means to miss the mark, and Satan is trying to convince you that God can't use you anymore. Satan is a deceiver, and whatever He is trying to convince you of, remember that the opposite is true.

Satan comes to condemn, but the Holy Spirit comes to convict. Condemnation connects you to your failure while conviction connects you to your identity. Condemnation tells you who you are not. Conviction tells you who you are. You need to settle in your heart that you have been forgiven. The forgiveness of God silences the voice of your accuser, Satan. In fact, you live in a state of forgiveness.

This does not mean that you no longer need to repent. Repentance is acknowledging you have missed the mark and need to do a course correction. I repent every day, constantly making course corrections in my thinking, habits, and lifestyle. When you have an unrepentant heart, you are measuring yourself by yourself instead of by the standard of Christ. First John 1:9 (KJ21) says, "If we confess our sins, He is faithful and just to forgive us our sins, and to cleanse us from all unrighteousness."

Second, Jesus canceled all the legal demands against us. This is another vital truth to understand if we are going to stand strong in the time of battle. This legal demand was the Old Testament law. Under the law, our sins were being imputed to us. In fact, according to Romans 5:13, "for until the Law sin was in the world, but sin is not counted against *anyone* when there is no law" (emphasis added). This text shows that sin is only imputed when the law is enforced. So under the law, Satan was using it as a weapon of condemnation.

Under the new covenant, our sins are imputed to Christ. This means Jesus fulfilled the righteousness of the law, freeing us from its judgment. When Jesus dealt with our sin on the cross, He stripped Satan of his power by removing the legal demands Satan used against us. The only way Satan can gain a legal right in your life is when you forfeit your rights as a child of God by rejecting the atoning sacrifice of Christ. This is a beautiful revelation to have. Satan has no right to judge and condemn us because we stand righteous because of what Jesus accomplished on our behalf.

"He made Him who knew no sin to be sin in our behalf, so that we might become the righteousness of God in Him" (2 Corinthians 5:21). In Christ, we stand completely righteous, independent of our performance, because it is a gift of His grace. So under the law, we got what we deserved, but under grace, we get what Jesus deserves.

In 2005, I had several drug charges pending against me. At the time of my court appearance, I had just gone through a radical transformation with Christ about a month prior. I had become a born-again believer and a new creation. I was from a small town where the judge knew me very well. The last time I saw him, that judge told me that if I ever came before him again in court, he would make me serve time. So needless to say, I was not looking forward to this court appearance.

My father happened to take me to court that day. As I stood before the judge, he said, "William, I've been looking forward to seeing you so that I can finally make you serve time in prison." Then he said, "However, I have been informed that the police department has lost the evidence it had to charge you with." I was in total shock and couldn't believe what I was hearing. Then the judge said, "I will fine you $666.00 dollars."

My dad stood up and said to the judge, "I will pay his debt in full." With those words, I was fully released from all the legal demands the court had against me that day. In the same way, when Jesus bled out on that cross, He paid your debt and settled all legal demands Satan had against you. This truth will set you free!

The third way Jesus disarmed the spiritual forces of wickedness was to remove our sin nature by nailing it to the cross. Our individual acts of sin are not what made us sinners. Our sin nature made us sinners, and Satan took advantage of that. "For as through the one man's disobedience the many were made sinners, so also through the obedience of the One the many will be made righteous" (Romans 5:19).

This clearly states that we received the sin nature from Adam, independent of our performance. In like manner, when we were born again, we received a righteous nature from Christ, independent of our performance. He did this by dying in our place.

Not only did Jesus die for you; He died *as* you on the cross. This means you were co-crucified with Christ. When you look at the cross, it should be a reminder of the price Jesus paid to set you free. Consider this passage from Romans:

> Or do you not know that all of us who have been baptized into Christ Jesus have been baptized into His death? Therefore we have been buried with Him through baptism into death, so that as Christ was raised from the dead through the glory of the Father, so we too might walk in newness of life. For if we have become united with Him in the likeness of His death, certainly we shall also be in the likeness of His resurrection, knowing this, that our old self was crucified with Him, in order that our body of sin might be done away with, so that we would no longer be slaves to sin; for he who has died is freed from sin.
>
> Romans 6:3–7 NASB95

In these verses, Paul clearly states that we have been co-crucified and co-resurrected with Christ. The sin nature is referred to as the body of sin in this text. So in this way, Jesus has removed the stumbling block of our sin nature, making the way for us to walk in total freedom from the power of sin and the devil.

The fourth way Jesus disarmed the spiritual forces of wickedness was to strip Satan from his place of power over your life. This is why the devil spends so much time trying to usurp it back through his deception and temptation. The reality is, because of Jesus, you are already in the place of victory. You are not fighting for victory; you are fighting from victory. You can even say it this way—Satan is a victim of your victory! Understanding God's truths will awaken you to the Word of God and the victory of Christ.

We must be aware of three stages concerning the defeat of Satan.

1. Satan is defeated by the cross of Christ.
2. Satan is being defeated as the body of Christ (the church) appropriates the victory of the cross. Satan is bound but still able to prowl around, using deception, temptation, and possession of the unredeemed.
3. Satan will be defeated by the return of Christ.

These three stages are the context we need in order to stand strong in the Lord in the midst of battle. Deception and temptation are Satan's weapons. They are all he has. Our job is to resist his lies and sinful nature, and when we do, the devil will run from us. In Ephesians 6:13, Scripture emphasizes the responsibility we have to take up the armor of God. "Therefore, take up the full armor of God, so that you will be able to resist on the evil day, and having done everything, to stand firm."

Satan is only interested in people he can influence. When he comes to your house and finds a submitted son or daughter of God, James 4:7 (NASB95) says he will flee. "Submit therefore to God. Resist the devil and he will flee from you." If Satan is constantly running *to* you, then you may be giving him a place of influence in your life. Obviously, this isn't always the case. Satan is a thief, and a thief doesn't look for permission to break in. Just because you are being attacked doesn't mean you are doing something that is granting him access. He is simply trying to break into your life illegally. However, because of the blood of Jesus that covers you, Satan doesn't have legal rights in your life.

Truth #3: "Stand firm therefore, having girded your loins with truth, and having put on the breastplate of righteousness" (Ephesians 6:14 NASB95) .

As we go through the armor of God, notice that all the pieces of the armor are protective by nature except one piece, which is an offensive weapon. Keep this in mind as we progress so that you will be able to follow my line of thinking. We will need to unpack two very important points, namely truth and righteousness, in verse 14.

Truth

If we were ever in a time where we needed an emphasis on truth, it is now. Living in the information age means we are bombarded with many different voices coming at us simultaneously every day. It can be very overwhelming, especially when lies and truth are so intermingled that it's hard to discern what is true from what is false. We are surrounded with so many platforms—news, social media, and entertainment—that give a voice to anything and anyone. However, we also have one constant in our midst that never changes: the Word of God.

John 1:1 says, "In the beginning was the Word, and the Word was with God, and the Word was God." In other words, truth is personified in the person of Jesus. He is the source of truth, and all truth comes from who He is. What this means is, in order for us to be a people of truth, we first must be a pursuer of Christ. We cannot afford to only pursue Jesus once a week at a church service. Television, social media, music—all of it never stops because Satan's agenda is to drown out Jesus as the voice of truth with non-stop noise.

Many years back, the Lord asked me to fast from media and television for forty days. The first four days were torture for me because at that time, all I did was watch TV. I remember thinking, *I don't have time to read the Bible.* As the fast progressed, my eyes were opened to just how much time I was giving to other voices in my life. I also began to realize that the movies I was watching were full of murder, lust, addiction, and sex. No wonder my emotions were constantly a mess!

Once I realized this, I made a commitment to devote all the time I would have been watching TV to reading the Bible instead. At the end of the fast, my mind was clear, my emotions were stable, and my faith was strengthened.

Many years later, I still honor that commitment to pursue the Word of truth, the Bible. As believers, we are called to reflect the stability of God's truth in society. How can we be a stable people in society if we fill ourselves with the voices of the world instead of Jesus, the voice of truth?

Scripture tells us that walking in God's truth produces fruit. "Jesus was saying to those Jews who had believed Him, 'If you continue in My word, then you are truly My disciples; and you will know the truth, and the truth will set you free'" (John 8:31–32). Jesus sets the context here with the statement, "If you continue in My word." What Jesus says next will really hit home: "And you will know the truth, and the truth will set you free."

> Satan enjoys ignorant Christians. As God's people, we can no longer afford to be ignorant of the truth of Christ.

Jesus's words are truth, and the more you spend time with His truths, the more you will understand and embrace them. Much of the bondage we experience is a byproduct of a lie believed. Therefore, bondage will dwell where truth is absent. The lifeline of a lie is ignorance or lack of understanding. That means that next to Satan, ignorance is the biggest threat to our God-given destiny and the greatest ally of Satan. Satan enjoys ignorant Christians. As God's people, we can no longer afford to be ignorant of the truth of Christ. How do we know we are believing a lie if we don't have the truth to expose it? God's truth protects us from the lies of Satan by exposing them.

Righteousness

The second part of verse 14 of Ephesians 6 speaks of the breastplate of righteousness. Here, let's reemphasize that every piece of the armor is God's armor; in other words, every piece represented comes from who He is. With this in mind, you can now settle in your heart that you are covered by the righteousness of Christ. Another term for righteousness is "right standing." In other words, we are able to advance the kingdom of God in warfare, according to the right standing of Jesus. Understanding this is vital in spiritual warfare.

In his letter to the church in Corinth, Paul says, "He made Him who knew no sin to be sin in our behalf, so that we might become the righteousness of God in Him" (2 Corinthians 5:21). We have become the righteousness of God in Christ. Our right standing with Father God is a direct result of the faithfulness of Jesus on our behalf. Since we are in Christ, we can live according to the benefits of His faithfulness. Jesus came to fulfill for us what we could not fulfill for ourselves, establishing our right standing.

Let's dive a little deeper into the aspect of righteousness:

But now apart from the Law the righteousness of God has been manifested, being witnessed by the Law and the Prophets, even the righteousness of God through faith in Jesus Christ for all those who believe; for there is no distinction; for all have sinned and fall short of the glory of God, being justified as a gift by His grace through the redemption which is in Christ Jesus; whom God displayed publicly as a propitiation in His blood through faith. This was to demonstrate His righteousness, because in the forbearance of God He passed over the sins previously committed; for the demonstration, I say, of His righteousness at the present time, so that He would be just and the justifier of the one who has faith in Jesus.

Romans 3:21–26 NASB95

Our righteousness has nothing to do with our own efforts or works. Our right standing with God comes through placing our faith in Jesus. Because we all have sinned and fallen short, no one can boast in his or her own righteous acts. We are made righteous as a gift of grace through Christ's faithfulness on our behalf. By placing our faith in Jesus, we are put right.

Here is another passage to consider. "For as through the one man's disobedience the many were made sinners, even so through the obedience of the One the many will be made righteous" (Romans 5:19). Here, we see the contrast between Adam and Christ. Through one man's disobedience (Adam), many were made sinners. As a result, we all are born with a sinful nature. Jesus came to restore our right standing with God by taking upon Himself our sin. When we are born again, we take upon ourselves the nature of Christ. So in the same way we are born sinners, we are reborn righteous by faith in Christ.

The question now becomes, "Who do you have faith in, Adam or Christ?" Most people have more faith in the fall of Adam than they do in the resurrection of Jesus. As a result, they are empowering a sin nature that is no longer part of their identity instead of empowering the righteous nature they were reborn with.

I was once at a Bible study, and a man there fell on the ground, manifesting a demon. He was growling, barking, and foaming at the mouth. Everyone in the study was freaked out and didn't know what to do. They were not just scared of the demon but of the man because he was also known for being very violent. The Lord had been teaching me about demons and casting them out, so I knelt down on the floor to cast the demons out of this man.

When he made eye contact with me, the demons started laughing and calling out all these different types of sins and accusing me of different things. It threw me off, and I immediately started doing a self-evaluation. When the demons realized I was focusing on my own righteousness apart from Christ, the battle got more intense. This went on for over an hour. Then I realized that I was trying to deal with the demons based on who I was apart from Jesus. Once I realized the enemy's trick and refocused on who I was in Christ, the demons came out a few minutes later as my pastor and I commanded them to leave.

> We are in right standing because of who Jesus is, not because of who we are. When we advance the kingdom, it is based on the work Jesus has done on our behalf.

This story shows that we are in right standing because of who Jesus is, not because of who we are. When we advance the kingdom, it is based on the work Jesus has done on our behalf. His righteousness protects us in the battle. The devil acknowledges His right standing.

This is key to remember! By the way, I realized later that all the sins the demons were accusing me of were from my past. Satan will speak to you from your past to create cycles of destruction.

PRAYER

Lord Jesus, I ask that You help me fully see and embrace what You have accomplished on the cross. I posture my heart to partner with the truth of what Your Word says about my victory in You. I thank You that through You, I am victorious. In Jesus's name.

WEAPONS FOR THE BATTLE

1. What you think will determine the direction of your life. You will not fall into any sin you didn't first meditate on. Taking every thought captive to Christ is essential to walking out freedom. Ask God to specifically speak to you regarding at least one area of your thought life that has believed a lie. (Suggestions might be financial, health [physical or mental], anger, lust, or fear. Or He might speak to you about another area.) Find at least three specific verses to stand against that lie. Stand on those verses until you have victory in this area.

2. Most people defeat themselves by the way they talk about themselves, whether or not they verbalize those words. But every part of your body responds to what you speak. If you are constantly speaking negative

things about yourself (whether out loud or silently), the rest of your being will adapt to that. If you speak positively about yourself, your being will respond to that. Eliminate the negative internal dialogue that is creating strongholds within your soul, and increase positive internal dialogue, which creates freedom within your soul. Ask God to help you catch yourself when you engage in negative self-talk. Replace that with positive self-talk.

3. Realize you are in a spiritual battle and the armor God has given you is for that battle. Gaining understanding of each piece of armor will equip you with the armor. Do a Bible study on the book of Ephesians. Or focus specifically on the armor of God discussed in Ephesians 6. Look into some of the historical uses of the pieces of the armor in Roman times. Compare those physical pieces to the spiritual use of the armor today.

8

THE GOSPEL IS OUR FIRM FOUNDATION

In Chapter 7, we covered three of the seven specific foundational truths listed in Ephesians 6 that we need to be aware of. We will be focusing on the next three truths in this chapter. With that, let's dive right in.

Truth #4: "And having shod your feet with the preparation of the gospel of peace" (Ephesians 6:15 NASB95).

Gospel of Peace

The gospel, or "good news," as it is often referred to, is the revelation of Jesus Christ. This revelation brings peace to our minds and hearts and gives us hope in the midst of darkness, providing direction where there is no visible path. To walk in peace in the battles of life, we need to be fully immersed in the gospel of peace or, better yet, the person of peace, Jesus Christ. The gospel of peace in Scripture mainly deals with God in relation to humankind. This means that because of what Jesus has accomplished on our behalf, we are saved from the wrath of God.

> But God demonstrates His own love toward us, in that while we were still sinners, Christ died for us. Much more then, having now been justified by His blood, we shall be saved from the wrath of God through Him. For if while we were enemies we were reconciled to God through the death of His Son, much more, having been reconciled, we shall be saved by His life.
>
> Romans 5:8–10

Most of the time, when looking at this text, we tend to only highlight verse 8 to show that Christ died for the sinner. Even though that is a tremendous truth that needs to be highlighted, that is not Paul's main point here. He was emphasizing the next two verses by stating "much more then." He was basically saying that if God loved you so much to die for you as a sinner, how much more does He love you now that you are His child?

Verse 9 goes on to state that because we have been justified by the blood of Christ, we are saved from the wrath of God. In other words, Jesus has taken upon Himself the wrath of God poured out on our sin so that now God the Father can relate to us unhindered. God is not dealing with you as a sinner but as a son.

In verse 10, Paul says again "much more," confirming that this is an unchangeable truth and summing it up with this profound statement that we are saved by the life of Christ. So again, God is not pouring out His wrath and anger on us, but we are now living in the time of grace. "Namely, that God was in Christ reconciling the world to Himself, not counting their wrongdoings against them, and He has committed to us the word of reconciliation" (2 Corinthians 5:19).

So what does this have to do with the armor of God and standing against the devil? It has a tremendous amount to do with it. Let me put it this way. If you don't understand that you are at peace with God and that He is at peace with you (see Romans 5:1), Satan will constantly attack your understanding of the goodness of God as it relates to you. In other words, Satan delights in the fact that he can cause you to credit his work to God because of poor beliefs.

One of the major access points of the demonic in the church today is a poor understanding of the goodness of God, particularly in this area of the gospel of peace. If Satan can distort your view of a good God, then he can devour your life (see 1 Peter 5:8). So we need to look to the person of Jesus to discover who God is in relation to us. Think about it this way—Jesus came to reveal the exact nature of God to us (see Hebrews 1:3), so whenever you are confused about His nature, look to the person of Jesus, who is an exact representation of God, and you will see the nature of God.

> Jesus came to reveal the exact nature of God to us, so whenever you are confused about His nature, look to the person of Jesus, who is an exact representation of God, and you will see the nature of God.

One of my favorite passages of Scripture that encapsulates the gospel of peace is Romans 5:1: "Therefore, since we have been justified by faith, we have peace with God through our Lord Jesus Christ" (CSB). Paul is saying that as we put faith in what Christ has done on our behalf, we can settle in our hearts that we have been justified or made right with God. The gift of grace empowers us to have confidence in our relationship before God. And not only are we in right standing with God; He is at total peace toward us—not angry with us or holding grudges against us—because of what Jesus accomplished on the cross. This is really good news!

When my wife, Chantal, was sixteen, a spirit of fear and anxiety came over her during the night. She could feel the demonic spirits tormenting her in her chest. As she lay there, God's Spirit came upon her and brought His peace, and the demonic spirits left. How good our God is to care for us so lovingly. Some people might hear this story and think that God afflicted her with those demons to teach her a lesson. That type of thinking is flawed. We should never allow people or Satan to convince us that God is an angry God. We are reconciled to God in Christ.

Truth #5: "In addition to all, taking up the shield of faith with which you will be able to extinguish all the flaming arrows of the evil one" (Ephesians 6:16).

As you see from this verse, faith protects us from the flaming arrows of Satan. Therefore, it follows that if faith protects, then unbelief exposes. This concept is not popular in today's Christianity. Be that as it may, we don't have the privilege of changing the way the kingdom of God functions. Faith is our part to play within the plan and purposes of God. With that being said, we need to lay a foundation of what new covenant faith consists of and how Satan tries to pervert it to gain access in our lives. For our faith to make an impact, it must be active. I like to break faith into three actionable parts: faith receives, faith discovers, and faith releases.

Faith Receives

When studying faith in the new covenant, let's start with Ephesians 2:8 (NASB95). "For by grace you have been saved through faith; and that not of yourselves, it is the gift of God." Faith works within a covenant of grace. Grace and faith are two sides of the same coin and should never be separated one from another. Yet within the body of Christ today, these concepts are rarely two discussed together. In this verse, Paul is showing us the function of grace as well as the posture of faith— grace provides and faith receives (what grace provides). The kingdom of God (salvation) cannot be achieved. It can only be received by faith. Salvation is a gift of grace to be faithfully received like a child. The same way you receive salvation is the way you receive the entirety of the kingdom of God—by faith.

Mark tells us more about this posture of faith. "Therefore, I say to you, all things for which you pray and ask, believe that you have received them, and they will be granted you" (Mark 11:24). Most people believe they have received when they see the answer to their prayers instead of when they pray. The posture of faith Mark is talking about operates from the place of completion.

This kind of faith does not believe something will happen but that something has already happened. How different would your prayer life be if you had this posture of faith? I propose that you would see a lot more of what you have asked for. Take the story of the woman with the issue of bleeding in Mark 5. Scripture says that she had hemorrhaged for twelve years and spent all her money seeking help from doctors, all to no avail. Then she heard about Jesus healing people.

> After hearing about Jesus, she came up in the crowd behind Him and touched His cloak. For she thought, "If I just touch His garments, I will get well." Immediately the flow of her blood was dried up; and she felt in her body that she was healed of her affliction. . . . And He said to her, "Daughter, your faith has made you well; go in peace and be healed of your affliction."
>
> Mark 5:27–29, 34 NASB95

Notice this woman's heart attitude—*I will receive it if I put myself in the right place*. She went and touched His garment, and the miracle took place. Her faith didn't move Jesus to her; it moved her to Jesus. Faith moved her into a place of receiving what Jesus was giving. Faith is about us moving into a place of receiving, not about moving God into a place of giving.

So what trick does Satan use to pervert our faith? His aim is to get us to see faith as something we do to get God to do something on our behalf. This mentality is detrimental to our faith because it focuses on what we do for God instead of what Christ has already done for us. This mentality will say things like, "I know God will bless me because I have been fasting and praying for forty days. I know God will bless me because I have been serving faithfully in the church for thirty years. I know God will bless me because I . . ." The focus in these statements is *self*. God does not move because of you but because of *Him*! God blesses you because He is good and righteous, not because you are.

I learned this principle the hard way. For years, I would pray for hours a day, begging and pleading with God to send revival to my city. Then one day, He told me that He was more willing to move in my city than I was willing to be a witness in my city. Immediately, I understood that He had already moved in the person of Christ and all I needed to do was align my faith to receive what He had already provided by His grace. Please do not misunderstand my point. I'm not saying to sit on the couch and not pray or fast or to do nothing. I'm just saying to do those things as directed by God because God is not the one stuck.

> God does not move because of you but because of *Him*! God blesses you because He is good and righteous, not because you are.

Faith Discovers

Imagine someone giving you an expensive computer that had every feature possible to make life easier. Now, imagine that you never took the time to discover all the different features. How useful will that computer be? It will only be useful to you to the degree you discover its features. You and I have been given the kingdom of God as a gift. This kingdom contains within it everything we need for life. However, if we never take the time to discover all that comes with the kingdom, how useful will it be?

For example, look at Ephesians 1:3. "Blessed be the God and Father of our Lord Jesus Christ, who has blessed us with every spiritual blessing in the heavenly places in Christ." Clearly, we have every spiritual blessing in the heavenly places in Christ. Notice that this passage emphasizes *every* and also the spiritual realm (heavenly places), which means that these realities abide in our spirits. So how should this affect the way we believe? It should cause us to think from provision instead of from lack. The Christian life is a never-ending journey of discovering what we already have in Christ (the Spirit). "For as many as are the promises of God, in Him they are yes; therefore also through Him is our Amen to the glory of God through us" (2 Corinthians 1:20 NASB95).

All the promises of God find their yes in Christ—they are fulfilled in Jesus. Therefore, the more I discover who Jesus is, the more I discover promises fulfilled in my life. We often make the mistake of separating the promises of God from the person of Jesus. When we do this, we begin to pursue promises instead of fellowship with the one who fulfills His promises. The promises of God then become goals of achievement instead of desires fulfilled in Christ. The pursuit of Jesus is the ultimate discovery of everything the kingdom contains. This does not mean that we don't pursue the promises. It means we pursue them through Christ.

Most of the Christian life is simply a discovery of what you already have in Christ. Here is how the apostle Peter puts it: "His divine power has granted to us everything pertaining to life and godliness, through the true knowledge of Him who called us by His own glory and excellence" (2 Peter 1:3). Since everything is already supplied by His grace, faith simply responds by receiving, discovering, and releasing its reality through our lives. In other words, the promises of God find their Amen through our lives.

The discovery aspect of faith is connected to the knowledge of Christ. The major stumbling blocks to our promises are ignorance and unbelief. Unbelief results in failure to receive. You may have knowledge but still need the faith to believe and to receive. Any area of our lives where there is lack is a knowledge issue. One of the most profound revelations I have ever received is when I realized that I was my own problem, not the devil. So I am the one that needs to pay attention to what Scripture reiterates. If God thinks it is important enough to say multiple times, then we should pay attention.

> Most of the Christian life is simply a discovery of what you already have in Christ. Since everything is already supplied by His grace, faith simply responds by receiving, discovering, and releasing its reality through our lives.

So what is the tactic of Satan in this area of faith? To convince you that you don't have what the Bible says you have. Satan delights in the fact you live ignorant of what you have in Jesus. Have you ever lost your car keys, only to find them in your pocket? That is the prayer life of most Christians. They spend all their time praying for things they already have in Christ. Ultimately, they are praying for God to give them what He has already provided. The moment Satan sees that you don't understand the finished work of the cross, he jumps all over you simply because you have put yourself in a defeated position by not discovering or realizing what you already have. If you don't understand you already have victory, you will spend all your days fighting for it.

Faith Releases

Faith releases the reality of what it has received and discovered in the Spirit. So if that is true, how do I release what I already have in the Spirit into the natural? First, it begins with the renewing of your mind. Picture a faucet. That faucet has a valve that determines the flow of the water. In your faith life, the valve is to your beliefs what the water flow is to the Spirit. The flow or release of the Spirit through your life is contingent upon your beliefs. What you believe will either release or quench the flow of the Spirit. Romans 12:2 clearly states that the renewing of the mind determines how the will of God is displayed through your life. This is probably the single greatest stumbling block for most Christians in regard to releasing the Spirit.

> What you believe will either release or quench the flow of the Spirit.

After coming out of a lifestyle of drugs and alcohol, I knew that major areas in my life needed to change after my salvation experience. Thankfully, I started attending a church that emphasized the renewing of the mind according to the authority of Scripture. To be honest, I was preparing myself to go through years of tedious healing of the heart. However, to my surprise, as I started renewing my mind according to Scripture, character flaws and sin issues rapidly disappeared. My pastors also noticed the radical changes in me and my increased desire to pursue God. I now recognize what was taking place. As I renewed my mind daily, I was releasing the power of the Spirit in my life. Romans 8:6 says that the mind set on the flesh is death, but the mind set on the Spirit is life and peace. Notice that our mindset determines what we will experience.

In addition to the renewing of your mind, faith is also released through the words we speak. Remember, the spirit realm functions by human agreement. What we come into agreement with is what we will experience. Here is how Jesus explains this concept:

> And Jesus answered saying to them, "Have faith in God. Truly I say to you, whoever says to this mountain, 'Be taken up and cast into the sea,' and does not doubt in his heart, but believes that what he says is going to happen, it will be granted him. Therefore I say to you, all things for which you pray and ask, believe that you have received them, and they will be granted you."
>
> Mark 11:22–24 NASB95

Notice from this passage that whatever is spoken in faith is manifested. In fact, Scripture says in Proverbs 18:21 that life and death are in the power of the tongue, and they that love it will eat the fruit thereof. For years, I tried to get around this fact until I came to the realization that the words we speak will generally be the world we experience. If you spend the majority of your day complaining, you will become more aware of things that entice you to complain. On the flip side, if you spend the majority of your day celebrating life, you will become more aware of things that make you thankful.

Why not align your voice to the Word of God? Imagine what your daily life experience would be if you simply shifted what you spoke to release the reality of the Spirit through your life. "It is the Spirit who gives life; the flesh profits nothing; the words that I have spoken to you are spirit and are life" (John 6:63 NASB95). The words of Christ were so impactful because they came from the Spirit.

The third way in which faith releases is through our actions. James says faith without works is dead.

> What use is it, my brethren, if someone says he has faith but he has no works? Can that faith save him? If a brother or sister is without clothing and in need of daily food, and one of you says to them, "Go in peace, be warmed and be filled," and yet you do not give them what is necessary for their body, what use is that? Even so faith, if it has no works, is dead, being by itself.
>
> James 2:14–17 NASB95

We are not called to simply acknowledge a need and speak a blessing. We also need to be an action expressing itself through love. Galatians 5:6 says that faith works through love. We do not work for faith; we work because we are a people of faith, and in doing so, we release the reality of the Spirit through our lives. Jesus also decreed that He did not come to do His own will but to do the will of the One that sent Him (see John 6:38). Therefore, Jesus's actions came from the reality of the Spirit. Our faith finds its completion through actions. So what tactics does Satan use to stop the release of the Spirit in our lives?

First, he attacks the mind through false beliefs. His main agenda is to keep the water valve turned off so that the Spirit is held captive within the believer. The Spirit of God is quenched through the unrenewed mind or false beliefs.

Second, Satan populates your words with gossip, slander, cursing, etc. "Let no unwholesome word proceed from your mouth, but only such a word as is good for edification according to the need of the moment, so that it will give grace to those who hear" (Ephesians 4:29 NASB95). Clearly, we are to talk in a way that edifies and builds up.

Third, Satan aims to hinder our godly actions so as to render us complacent in our witness of the gospel because the devil finds his identity when we do not live out our sonship. When we are disobedient to the prompting of the Spirit, we are quenching the flow of the Spirit. Each of us must decide for ourselves whether the Spirit lives within to be *our* servant or for us to be *His* servant.

Truth #6: And take the helmet of salvation and the sword of the Spirit, which is the word of God" (Ephesians 6:17).

We must properly understand salvation if we are to stand strong against the schemes of Satan. Salvation is the foundation of our Christian life. If Satan can crack the foundation of salvation, then everything else in life becomes shaky. Throughout our Christian journey, Satan will come back to this issue of salvation over and over. His main objective is that we focus on a works-based salvation, so he tries to convince us that our salvation is a result of works—of what we do. He wants us to think that our works give us salvation and also enable us to keep our salvation.

Ephesians 2:8 says, "For by grace you have been saved through faith; and this is not of yourselves, it is the gift of God." Did you catch that? Salvation is a gift of grace. We can do nothing to achieve salvation. It can only be received by faith. This truth needs to be settled in our thinking because this is where the devil attacks. The apostle Paul goes on to say, "Not as a result of works, so that no one may boast. For we are His workmanship, created in Christ Jesus for good works, which God prepared beforehand so that we would walk in them" (Ephesians 2:9–10).

Salvation is based solely on the work of Christ. As a result of our salvation, however, we are able to embrace the work God created us for. Salvation is twofold in this regard—we are saved from a work to be restored to a work. It is a delusion of grace to think salvation is a liberation to live free from obedience to God. In fact, Paul said this in 1 Corinthians 15:10: "But I labored even more than all of them, yet not I, but the grace of God with me." Grace is a divine enablement to live according to the works of our created purpose.

When Paul tells us to take up the helmet of salvation, he is telling us that we must protect our minds regarding God's truth about salvation. The next time Satan brings up your failures or attacks your salvation, remind him of what the Word of God says in Psalm 103:12 (NASB95): "As far as the east is from the west, so far has He removed our transgressions from us." The only person who can strip your salvation from you is you by your willful rejection of Christ as Savior. When someone becomes apostate, their conscience is completely seared, and they don't even care that they have rejected Christ. That is not you!

The second part of Ephesians 6:17 tells us to take up the sword of the Spirit, which is the Word of God. The Word of God is the only offensive weapon we have in our armor because it is divinely capable of destroying the works of Satan. As you utilize the Word of God for your warfare, you are building within you an unshakable foundation of beliefs, habits, lifestyle, and ultimately, destiny. Far too often, people sadly fail to utilize the weapon of the Word of God when battling in the Spirit. If the Word of God is your weapon, that means your voice is the avenue through which that weapon flows. To wield the sword of the Spirit is to align your voice with the Word of God. According to Scripture, your voice is very significant.

James 1:26 says, "If anyone thinks himself to be religious, yet does not bridle his tongue but deceives his own heart, this person's religion is worthless." What a powerful but sobering statement.

If we are to be effective in standing against Satan, we must learn to bridle our tongue because Satan is empowered when we speak in agreement with his purposes. We neglect to watch ourselves in this important area. An unbridled tongue participates in ungodly behavior through conversations and comments that are not in alignment with the nature of God. James goes on to say,

> So also the tongue is a small part of the body, and yet it boasts of great things. See how great a forest is set aflame by such a small fire! And the tongue is a fire, the very world of iniquity; the tongue is set among our members as that which defiles the entire body, and sets on fire the course of our life, and is set on fire by hell.
>
> James 3:5–6 NASB95

Read this passage again. Did you catch what James is saying? The tongue is the very world of iniquity, and when unbridled, it defiles the body because it empowers the forces of wickedness. Your tongue may be small, but the words you speak carry great power for either the kingdom of God or Satan.

Many of the issues I have faced in life have been a byproduct of an unbridled tongue that allowed the forces of wickedness to set the blaze of destruction. For example, in the region where I grew up, the unbridled tongue is one of the major cultural issues and manifests as complaining, gossiping, and slander. It seems almost normal for that area. However, a byproduct of this is a lot of drunkenness, brokenness, depression, suicide, and more.

Once I became a born-again believer and started attending church, I noticed that the same culture that was in the world is also in the church. I realized that I spent most of the day complaining or gossiping about people. Once I recognized what I was doing, I determined that I would not continue to allow the world around me to determine my behavior and speech anymore. I started practicing with my friends, and we changed our conversation every time it became negative.

To my astonishment, our conversations gradually became more and more godly. Over the years, when people get around me, they stop talking in certain ways simply because they respect me. The unbridled tongue is a major area of warfare, and we generally do not notice that it is killing us daily.

God calls us to be a solution—not a problem—in the world. Jesus has this to say about our speech: "It is not what enters into the mouth that defiles the man, but what proceeds out of the mouth, this defiles the man" (Matthew 15:11 NASB95). Your voice is so powerful, it can either play a role in freedom or bondage for you and others. You must never allow your voice to be a weapon of destruction but rather an instrument of justice. Justice is about restoring things that are not right, which is what God intends to do through us.

> How blessed is the man who does not walk in the counsel of the wicked, nor stand in the path of sinners, nor sit in the seat of scoffers! But his delight is in the law of the LORD, and in His law he meditates day and night. He will be like a tree firmly planted by streams of water, which yields its fruit in its season and its leaf does not wither; and in whatever he does, he prospers.
>
> Psalm 1:1–3 NASB95

The Word of God provides everything you need in life to be fruitful. The major challenge is allowing the Word to be the authority that shapes what you believe and how you live. A life of barrenness is not part of the Christian life. God has provided everything you need to be fruitful in every season in life. In fact, God's words coming from your mouth actually equip you. "All Scripture is inspired by God and profitable for teaching, for reproof, for correction, for training in righteousness; so that the man of God may be adequate, equipped for every good work" (2 Timothy 3:16–17 NASB95).

All Scripture is empowered by the voice of God. When we speak forth the Word, we are speaking forth the authority of God within His Word. We must understand this truth if we are to stand in battle with confidence. We must know that when we speak forth the Word of God, we are not speaking forth the authority of man but the authority of God.

> For the word of God is living and active and sharper than any two-edged sword, and piercing as far as the division of soul and spirit, of both joints and marrow, and able to judge the thoughts and intentions of the heart.
>
> Hebrews 4:12 NASB95

In the garden, Satan came to Eve to undermine the Word of God. Everything the devil does is in opposition to what God has decreed as truth, which is why we need to know His truths. If the Word of God is sharper than any two-edged sword, then we must be familiar with this weapon of warfare. One side of this sword is designed to destroy the works of Satan while the other side is designed to establish the works of God. Many believers are not walking in freedom because of an ignorance of the sword they carry. Bondage increases in your life to the degree of your ignorance.

That is why I spend every day meditating on Scripture—so I am prepared with the right word for the moment of attack. For example, if I am sick, I do not want to use Scripture that has nothing to do with healing. When you fight with general words, you get general victories. You must realize that when Satan attacks, you need to fight with a word that is pertinent to that situation. If you are sick, that is not the time to quote that God will never leave or forsake you. That truth will bring comfort to the soul but will not provide a solution to the immediate problem. This is also not the time to simply confess you are healed. That is also truth, but it is not using the Word as a weapon but as comfort. You need to speak to the sickness and command it to leave. You are not a sick person trying to get healed. You are a healed person resisting sickness by using the Word to speak to it.

The Bible says that every word God speaks will always accomplish His purpose (see Isaiah 55:11). Any area in your life that is not fruitful is a place where the Word is not dominant. Learn to identify what God has decreed and then come into alignment with His purposes so that you can walk in the fullness of what is yours in the cross of Jesus Christ.

Again, the Word of God is your weapon of warfare. It is foolish to be ignorant of the Word because you will be engaging in battle without the needed offensive weapon. In fact, ignorance of the Word is like handing Satan our sword to use against us. This is the reality for most Christians that live defeated lives. It begins and ends with what we do with the Word in our minds, beliefs, attitudes, habits, and lifestyles.

PRAYER

Lord Jesus, I ask for greater grace to live according to biblical faith, the faith that receives from You. Please give me the faith that discovers all the promises we already have in You, the faith that moves me into obedience with Your promises by appropriating them in my life. In Jesus's name.

WEAPONS FOR THE BATTLE

1. Faith receives, discovers, and releases. List three things for each of these. For example, faith receives God's promise in the area of ____, ____, ____. Faith discovers the truth of God's Word in this area. And faith releases that promise of God's Word. Be as specific as possible here. Specific requests will result in specific answers.

2. Bridle your tongue by learning to control your emotions. Emotions are God-given, but they are not to be your leader since they change on a moment-by-moment basis. So learning to govern your emotions by what you fill your mind with is essential to bridling the tongue. Notice that when you spoke negatively, you did so in a moment when your emotions were out of control. A focus on having healthy emotions is essential to bridling the tongue.

   a. First, renew your mind with God's Word and bring your emotions under its dominion.

   b. Second, think before you speak. Most of the time when you say something that is unhealthy, it is because you spoke without thinking. Take a moment and think through all the times you said something before you fully thought about it. This should reveal the need to think before speaking.

c. Third, change your vocabulary. Learning a new way of communicating with people can greatly increase your awareness of what you say. The reality is that we all should be learning better ways to communicate with people. A concentrated effort of thinking about our words will greatly increase our ability to bridle the tongue.

9

AN EFFECTIVE PRAYER LIFE

We now come to the seventh and final truth of the seven specific foundational truths listed in Ephesians 6: praying at all times in the Spirit. We cannot overemphasize the importance of the need for prayer, especially in this hour.

Truth #7: "With all prayer and petition pray at all times in the Spirit, and with this in view, be on the alert with all perseverance and petition for all the saints" (Ephesians 6:18 NASB95).

As we conclude our examination of the armor of God and the significant role it plays in standing against the plans and schemes of Satan, I want to wrap up with a look at the importance of prayer. Every believer needs to build on the foundation of a vibrant prayer life in their relationship with God. Before we get into a deeper study on prayer, we first need to see the context of what prayer is.

Prayer is communication with God. While this definition is stating the obvious, the emphasis on communication makes the difference. To be a little more specific, prayer is about developing a relationship with God through our communication with Him. Outside of true relationship with God, we are just going through the motions of our beliefs without tapping into His riches. If prayer is about relationship, then how we communicate with God is very important.

Think about it in terms of your natural relationship with people. One of the top three things within a relationship that can cause conflict is poor communication or a lack of communication. If you only spoke to a family member once in a great while, you would not have a very good relationship because your lack of communication would invariably lead you both to make assumptions about each other. Once you begin to make assumptions, false beliefs are formed in your attitudes toward that person until your relationship is based on illusions instead of truth.

> Prayer is about developing a relationship with God through our communication with Him.

This happens to many people in their relationship with God. Poor communication or a lack of communication leads to assumptions about God. You can think you know what God thinks based on assumptions and miss what God actually thinks entirely. A. W. Tozer said, "What comes into our minds when we think about God is the most important thing about us."[1]

1. A. W. Tozer, *The Knowledge of God: The Attributes of God. Their Meaning in the Christian Life* (San Francisco: HarperCollins, 1961), 1.

The Fruitful Prayer Life

With this context in mind, let's turn to Scripture to deal with two specific areas—our beliefs and our motivations. God weighs both the thoughts and intentions of your heart. What you believe has a great deal to do with the fruitfulness of your prayer life. The motivations of your heart determine who is glorified by your actions. Let's begin in the book of Matthew and look at how Jesus taught us to pray. "Beware of practicing your righteousness before men to be noticed by them; otherwise you have no reward with your Father who is in heaven" (Matthew 6:1 NASB95).

Notice that Jesus addresses the issue of the heart before teaching how to pray. Jesus is looking for a specific heart motivation. He is not saying to stop practicing your righteousness before man. In the previous chapter, He says this:

> You are the light of the world. A city set on a hill cannot be hidden; nor does anyone light a lamp and put it under a basket, but on the lampstand, and it gives light to all who are in the house. Let your light shine before men in such a way that they may see your good works, and glorify your Father who is in heaven.
>
> Matthew 5:14–16 NASB95

Based on these verses, Jesus intends for us to practice our righteousness before man so that Father God is glorified by our lives. He wants to deal with the motivation of the heart—what is motivating us to practice our righteousness?

Matthew 6:1 says, "Do not practice your righteousness for the purpose of being noticed by man" (paraphrased). The motivation of the heart determines who is glorified by our actions. When the motivation of the heart is for others to notice us, we become the object of glorification.

Consider another passage from 1 Samuel 16:7 (NASB95). "But the LORD said to Samuel, 'Do not look at his appearance or at the height of his stature, because I have rejected him; for God sees not as man sees, for man looks at the outward appearance, but the LORD looks at the heart.'" God is looking at our heart in everything that we do. We may be able to fool man, but we cannot fool God. In fact, we can look reverent to God in the eyes of man while being irreverent to God by the condition of our heart. We must be aware of developing a life that appears reverent. Jesus is setting up this backdrop as He teaches on prayer. Let's continue to move through Matthew 6.

> So when you give to the poor, do not sound a trumpet before you, as the hypocrites do in the synagogues and in the streets, so that they may be honored by men. Truly I say to you, they have their reward in full. But when you give to the poor, do not let your left hand know what your right hand is doing, so that your giving will be in secret; and your Father who sees what is done in secret will reward you.
>
> Matthew 6:2–4 NASB95

In this passage, Jesus is addressing the condition of the heart by creating another contrast. He is not telling us not to give to the poor. He is simply addressing our motivation behind what we do. In verse 5, He goes on to say that when we give to be honored by man, we have our reward in full. This reveals our motivation. And the motivation of the heart determines the reward we receive. When our motivation is to be honored by man, our reward is based on man. When our motivation is to honor God, our reward is based on Him.

Jesus ends these verses by telling us to give in secret. Again, this doesn't mean not to let people know what you are doing. It means to do it from the secret motivation of your heart to honor God. In the eyes of God, the motivation of the heart is most important. Prayer is not about the attention of man but the attention of God.

> In the eyes of God, the motivation of the heart is most important. Prayer is not about the attention of man but the attention of God.

Your Prayer Closet

Once Jesus had the disciples' attention, He took prayer a step further:

> But you, when you pray, go into your inner room, close your door and pray to your Father who is in secret, and your Father who sees what is done in secret will reward you. And when you are praying, do not use meaningless repetition as the Gentiles do, for they suppose that they will be heard for their many words. So do not be like them; for your Father knows what you need before you ask Him.
>
> Matthew 6:6–8 NASB95

Again, Jesus is not saying to never pray in public. He is telling us that what pleases Father God is a heart that becomes a room for only Him. In that room, we do not have to pray with meaningless repetition to get His attention. We already have

His attention. In fact, He already knows what we need. Prayer is more than our needs being met. It's about relationship being established.

The Lord's Prayer

Pray, then, in this way: "Our Father, who is in heaven, hallowed be Your name. Your kingdom come. Your will be done, on earth as it is in heaven. Give us this day our daily bread. And forgive us our debts, as we also have forgiven our debtors. And do not lead us into temptation, but deliver us from evil. [For Yours is the kingdom and the power and the glory forever. Amen.]"

Matthew 6:9–13 NASB95

Through the Lord's Prayer as found in Matthew 6, Jesus begins to teach us how to approach God in prayer. In these verses, we see what Jesus's prayer life looked like and what He wants ours to look like. He begins in verse 9 by telling us how to view God—as our Father and our Lord who deserves to be honored as such. Why is it important to understand this twofold view? First, if we only view God as Father, we will never truly honor Him as Lord. Second, if we only view God as Lord, we will never truly see Him as Father. Jesus is giving us the proper lens to view God through—as Father God. This view brings together His Fatherhood and Godhead so that we approach Him as Father and live in reverence to Him as Lord.

Verse 10 gives us the heart of Father God in regard to our life within this world. Notice here the emphasis on the joining of heaven and earth. When you look at the biblical narrative beginning in Genesis 1–2 and ending in Revelation 21–22, it has never been about people leaving earth. The narrative has always been about the rule of God within this world. Over the years, the emphasis has been changed to a focus on leaving this world behind. Yet this emphasis is not consistent with the overall narrative of Scripture.

God intends for heaven and earth to be joined in union with one another. One of the ways He intends to do this is through His people in this world. Since it is God's intention to remake and reshape this world through us, that means our prayers need to be consistent with His narrative.

In this verse, notice the focus on a threefold prayer: God's kingdom coming to earth, God's will being done on earth, and heaven being established. When our prayers are not consistent with this narrative, we will not be effective in establishing the purposes of God. Obviously, the full consummation of this will not take place until the return of Christ. However, the beginnings of this have already started with the first coming of Christ. The heaven and earth initiative began with Jesus and continues through His people in the world.[2]

Verse 11 tells us that prayer is about recognizing Father God as the provider of everything in life. We can so easily form our prayer lives around what we think our needs are and exclude God from all other areas of life. We need God in everything, not just in our perceived needs. The heart posture necessary for a vibrant prayer life is to live in the realization of our need for God in every aspect of life.

Verse 12 addresses the issue of forgiveness. When we forget "that while we were still sinners, Christ died for us" (Romans 5:8), we judge the world in its sin through prayer. We have

2. For further study of this, read N. T. Wright's *Surprised by Hope* (New York: HarperOne, 2008).

not been given the ministry of judgment but of reconciliation (2 Corinthians 5:18–19). We are called to receive and release forgiveness. Christ came to reconcile the world back to God, and He has commissioned us with the same mission as His ambassadors. The core value of reconciliation is not counting people's trespasses against them. Jesus wants us to emphasize this in both our lives and our prayers. If we stand in prayer with judgment and accusation, we are coming into agreement with an antichrist spirit, which contributes to the brokenness around us. How we pray is either destroying darkness or partnering with it.

In verse 13, we find Jesus emphasizing that prayer is not about focusing on the temptation but on the God that delivers us from the temptation. Regardless of the situation, we need to acknowledge that God has a plan of deliverance. He has supreme authority and power. Prayer is about identifying God's faithful plan of deliverance from evil. First Corinthians 10:13 says that He will not allow us to be tempted beyond what we are able but will provide the way of escape so that we can endure. When our faith is in His faithfulness to provide a way out, we are positioned properly in prayer.

With this understanding of the Lord's Prayer, I want to end with a focus on the faithfulness of our loving Father God as found in Colossians 1:13. "For He rescued us from the domain of darkness, and transferred us to the kingdom of His beloved Son." This is a favorite passage of mine, especially in times of battle. The knowledge that we have been rescued is essential for a healthy prayer life. The cross has already won the victory over Satan, and we are here to enforce that victory over all his works. Prayer is about praying from a victorious position in Christ. This is what it means to be delivered from evil. We have

AN EFFECTIVE PRAYER LIFE

been delivered and will continue to be delivered until all God's enemies have been made His footstool.

This model of the Lord's Prayer encapsulates the Ephesians 6:18 narrative. We generally think praying in the spirit only means speaking in tongues, but it also means praying in alignment with heaven's agenda as found in the model prayer Jesus gave. This prayer also covers our approach to God for ourselves as well as for others. It ends with the victorious perspective of deliverance for any situation.

Before I started using this prayer model, I did not see a lot of fruit in my prayers. A lot of my praying was more focused on demons and calling out demons, which resulted in a lot of demonic activity in my home. I didn't realize that my focus on the demonic realm was actually opening doors to the presence of Satan in my home.

It all came to a head when a warlock started astral-projecting into my home, placing curses on me. All hell broke out in my home for several months. I didn't realize at the time that the way I was praying was strengthening the demonic activity because I was focusing on them through prayer. Demons started coming and holding me down in my bed at night. I would wake up in the morning with scratches all over my body. I thought that something had to be wrong with my prayer focus.

I've always understood that God is not my problem. So I didn't start blaming God for what was happening. I understood that God played a part and that I played a part in cooperation with Him. God had already given me everything I needed to walk in victory. It was just a matter of aligning myself with the weapons He gave me to walk it out. Once I started shifting the focus of my prayer and aligned myself to the purposes of God using the Lord's Prayer as my model, the warlock left my city, the demons stopped infiltrating my home, and divine encounters with God began. Since that time, I have walked in more freedom and victory than ever before.

Shortly after this battle, I went through a three-month encounter with the presence of God manifesting in my home as a cloud. At the time, I had a contract with a local pest control agency. One day, my phone rang. One of the employees wanted to talk to me about my home. He began to explain that every time he came into my house, a cloud of smoke was hovering all over. He could feel so much peace in my home that he didn't want to leave. He asked what the smoke was. I had an opportunity to minister to him about the God of peace he encountered in my home.

I have since realized that our homes are to be sanctuaries that host the presence of God. If Satan can infiltrate our homes, he can disrupt the place designed for safety and rest. Prayer begins in the home and creates the atmosphere there. What atmosphere are you creating?

Conclusion

My prayer for you is that after you have gone through this book, you will be more confident in walking out your life in the victory that is yours in Christ. I want to encourage you again with some of the truths we have studied together.

First, Satan is not a victor in your life. He only gets his power through human agreement.

Second, his tactics are deception and temptation. Understanding these two points and combating them effectively are keys to maintaining victory throughout your life.

Third, Christ abides within you by His Spirit. First John 4:4 says, "Greater is He who is in you than he who is in the world."

Fourth, you have everything you need to live victoriously already deposited into your spirit. Therefore, you are fully equipped to trample over every demon that comes your way.

Last, stay focused and encouraged by the victory of Christ. Remember that Satan is the victim of your victory in Christ!

Prayer

Lord, I ask that You help me cultivate intimate fellowship with You in prayer. I call upon Your grace in this area to be intentional about praying daily. Lord, give me the wisdom and understanding that I need to intercede on behalf of others. Lord, I thank You that through prayer, the mysteries of the kingdom will be released. In Jesus's name.

Weapons for the Battle

Develop a vibrant prayer life. Here is a helpful prayer model:

1. Prayer is simply communication with God. You need to remember that it is a dialogue not a monologue. Most people do all the talking in prayer and wonder why it's fruitless.
2. Listen in prayer. It may help to journal by asking God a question.
3. Write down an answer to the question. This will help you develop a dialogue with God. Compare your

answer to be sure it lines up with the whole of Scripture. This will help with discernment.

4. Develop a continual internal dialogue with God. Every one of us talks to ourselves all the time, so simply shift that dialogue to God. Prayer is not just about having a slotted time of the day where we pray out loud. It's also about ongoing internal fellowship with the Spirit.

A Global Awakening associate evangelist, **William Wood** is also a graduate of the Global School of Supernatural Ministry and founder of the Relentless conference. In 2005, William Wood had a dramatic encounter with God and was supernaturally delivered from alcohol and drug abuse. He now has a passion for revival and for seeing people step into the fullness of what Christ paid for on the cross. William longs to see the body of Christ come into the fullness of maturity.

As such, William focuses on equipping the saints for the work of ministry as mature sons and daughters as Jesus Himself was when He walked the earth. His passion is to see the fulfillment of the declaration Jesus made in John 14:12—that we would do the works He did and even greater.

William walks out this call as an itinerant minister and disciple maker, helping people step into their fullness by equipping churches around the world through conferences, training workshops, power evangelism, and missions. As he works with churches to develop their discipleship programs through focusing on Jesus's model of discipleship, they will then help to mature the body of Christ.

NOTES

NOTES

NOTES

NOTES

NOTES

NOTES

NOTES